# The Motherhood Mandate

*A SPECIAL ISSUE OF*

*PSYCHOLOGY OF WOMEN QUARTERLY*

*EDITED BY*

*NANCY FELIPE RUSSO*

**HUMAN SCIENCES PRESS**

72 Fifth Avenue    3 Henrietta Street
NEW YORK, NY 10011 ● LONDON, WC2E 8LU

HUMAN SCIENCES PRESS
72 Fifth Avenue
New York, New York 10011

Printed in the United States of America

**Library of Congress Cataloging in Publication Data**

Main entry under title:

The Motherhood mandate.

   (Psychology of women quarterly; v. 4, no. 1)
   Bibliography: p.
   1. Women—Psychology—Addresses, essays, lectures. 2. Sex role—Addresses, essays, lectures. 3. Mothers—United States—Addresses, essays, lectures. 4. Childlessness—United States—Psychological aspects—Addresses, essays, lectures. I. Russo, Nancy Felipe, 1943– II. Series.
HQ1206.P76 vol. 4, no. 1    301.41'2s [301.41'2]
ISBN 0-87705-463-0
LC: 79-88275

# CONTENTS

**VOLUME 4 NUMBER 1**                               **FALL 1979**

The **Psychology of Women Quarterly** is sponsored by Division 35 of the American Psychological Association. Empirical studies, critical reviews, theoretical articles, and invited book reviews are published in the *Quarterly*. Unusual findings in studies otherwise not warranting a full report may be written as brief reports. The kinds of problems addressed include: psychobiological factors, behavioral studies, role development and change, career choice and training, management variables, education, discrimination, therapeutic processes, and sexuality. These suggestions are not meant to be exhaustive, but rather to guide investigations in the psychology of women.

MANUSCRIPTS must be sent in triplicate to: Professor Georgia Babladelis, Editor, *Psychology of Women Quarterly*, Department of Psychology, California State University, Hayward, California 94542. Blind review procedures are used. Authors are responsible for preserving their anonymity in the pages of their manuscript. Style is according to the *APA Publication Manual*, 1974 revision. The *Publication Manual* is available in most departments or libraries or can be purchased from: American Psychological Association, 1200-17th Street, N.W., Washington, D.C. 20036. Authors should seek written permission from the copyright owner (usually the publisher) for the use of tables, illustrations, or extensively quoted material which has previously appeared in another publication. Articles are published in the order in which they are accepted. Provisions for early publication of an accepted article can be made if the author is willing to pay the cost of the extra pages required. No free reprints are available to the author, but reprints may be purchased from the publisher.

SUBSCRIPTIONS are on an academic year basis: $40 per year. Rates for individual professionals and students are available on request from the Business Office. ADVERTISING and subscription inquiries should be made to Human Sciences Press, 72 Fifth Avenue, New York, New York 10011. (212) 243-6000. Rates are available on request.

OVERSEAS SUBSCRIBERS: Human Sciences Press, 3 Henrietta Street, London, WC2E 8LU England.

INDEXED in Sociological Abstracts, Human Resources Abstracts, Psychological Abstracts, Social Sciences Citation Index, Current Contents/Social and Behavioral Sciences, Current Index to Journals in Education (CIJE), Chicorel Abstracts to Reading and Learning Disabilities, Child Development Abstracts and Bibliography, Development and Welfare (India), Human Sexuality Update, Marriage and Family Review.

L.C.: 76—12952            ISSN: 0361 6843            PWOQDY 4(1) 1-148 (1979)

# Editorial

Once again we inaugurate a new volume with a special issue: The Motherhood Mandate. Our guest editor, Nancy Felipe Russo, not only suggested this topic but also undertook all the responsibility for bringing it together for our readers.

Periodically I use this space to bring you up to date on our progress. We are beginning our fourth year of publication with the interest and support of our subscribers still strong. A recent survey of subscribers revealed that they like: range of articles, special issues, book and film reviews, and our open editorial policy which includes such things as rotation of consulting editors, open list for ad hoc reviewers and reception to new ideas. Many persons criticized us for our publication lag and some respondents expressed misgivings about the use of APA writing style and for not having more brief articles.

To date, we have received over 450 manuscripts. Our acceptance rate is about 30%. Approximately 90% of authors are university affiliated and about 10% have clinical affiliations. Half of our articles are single authored and half are multiple authored and most of the authors (75%) are women. In volume 3 we published two special issues (Dual career couples and Androgyny) and increased the number of brief articles as well. Steps have been taken to reduce publication lag. With the cooperation of our publisher, we will be increasing the size of the Quarterly with this volume by 50%. Naturally, the cost of such an increase will be reflected in higher subscription rates but we thought it would be worth it to readers and writers alike to have current articles available. Soon we will be publishing a list of accepted articles in the Division 35 Newsletter as well as information about special issues. Special issues nearing completion are: Women and work, and Women as patients. In progress are: Women as role models, Black Women, Sexuality, Middle age and aging, Relationships, and others.

My thanks to all the persons who responded to the survey and gave us the benefit of their observations. We hope all readers will feel free to write to us with their comments or suggestions. We have no doubt that you will find this special issue on sex roles and fertility stimulating and informative.

Georgia Babladelis
*California State University, Hayward*

# Overview: Sex Roles, Fertility and the Motherhood Mandate

Nancy Felipe Russo

*American Psychological Association*

Abstract: The centrality of motherhood to woman's identity is charac-terized as a mandate that is built into our social institutions as well as our psyches. This mandate is reflected in the assumptions of the models and methods of research in the psychology of women. An examination of the impact of the motherhood mandate is encouraged and complexities that must be reflected in research models and methods are underscored. These complexities include the need for (1) appreciation of the context of the phenomena studied; (2) interactionist approaches, including multivariate models and methods; and (3) a multidisciplinary perspective, including biological, psychological, social and structural levels of analysis. Two facets of the changing context having profound implications for the meaning of motherhood are reproductive freedom and voluntary childlessness.

The implications of the centrality of motherhood to woman's identity are not sufficiently appreciated by researchers in the field of the psychology of women. Motherhood is on a qualitatively different plane than other sex roles for women in our society. It is a mandate that pervades our social institutions as well as our psyches (Bernard, 1974).

Put simply, the mandate of motherhood in its traditional form

I would like to thank Georgia Babladelis, Susan Bram, Sharon Dyer. Murray Gendell, Alan Gross, Elaine Hilberman, Gloria Kamenske, Kathy Leser, Allen Meyer, Ann Miller, Howard Moss, Virginia O'Leary, Karen Paige, Joy Stapp, Sandra Tangri, Cheryl Travis, and Barbara Wall-ston for their assistance in the development of this issue of *The Psychology of Women Quarterly* devoted to sex roles and fertility. A special expression of thanks goes to Sharon Dyer and Allen Meyer. Without their assistance the issue would not have been possible. Thanks also go to the authors, whose cooperation and patience throughout the long process that a special issue in-volves is deeply appreciated. Requests for reprints of this overview should be sent to Nancy Felipe Russo, Women's Program, APA, 1200 17th Street, N.W., Washington, D.C. 20036.

requires that a woman have at least two children (historically as many as possible, and preferably sons), and raise them "well." She can, however, become educated, work, and be active in public life, as long as she first fulfills this obligation. The kicker in this scheme is the definition of "well." A "good" mother must be physically present to serve her infant's every need. As the child enters school, a mother may pursue other activities—but only those permitting her to be instantly available should her child "need" her (Russo, 1976).

Incompatibility with other roles is thus built into society's definition of good motherhood. No matter how well a woman manages multiple roles (e.g., mother and worker) she is in violation of the motherhood mandate and may face personal feelings of guilt and ostracism by family members, peers, and others. Both sexes must deal with society's reproductive ethic. But fatherhood has demanded that men participate in multiple roles to provide for their families. Only recently has conflict between filling a provider role and serving the needs of one's children emerged as an issue for men (Fein, 1978).

As early as 1916, Leta Hollingworth analyzed "social devices for impelling women to bear children," and provided examples of how this pronatalist bias in research on women contributed to such devices (Hollingworth, 1916). This bias continues to be reflected in our research. My purpose in assembling the articles in this issue is to encourage an examination of the motherhood mandate in the United States, and to suggest some of the complexities that must be reflected in our theories and methods if understanding of the interrelationships among sex role and fertility variables is to advance. Appreciation of such complexities requires recognition of the implications of the changing context for the meaning of motherhood.

## THE CONTEXT

Kearney reminds us that childbearing takes place in the context of a social structure that influences sex roles as well as fertility. The motherhood mandate continues to be used to justify institutional discrimination that denies females equal access to education, employment, insurance benefits, and credit (Russo, 1976). Ironically, reform efforts on behalf of women can work to women's detriment in the longer run if they increase institutionalized support for motherhood. To understand the processes involved we must examine the context that subtly and not-so-subtly influences the nature and meaning of childbearing in our society.

The women's movement has brought tremendous changes in the social structure, in sex role relationships, and in woman's concept of self. Three related facets of the changing context of motherhood that have profound implications for interrelationships among sex role and fertility variables and thus for our theories and methods are: (1) workforce participation of mothers; (2) reproductive freedom (i.e., the ability to control one's reproduction without coercion); and (3) voluntary childlessness.

## Workforce Participation of Mothers

In 1947, less than 1/3 of all women were in the workforce; in 1978, nearly 1/2 of all women were in the workforce. This dramatic increase in labor force participation is due almost entirely to change in the behavior of married women. In 1940, 15% of married women were employed outside the home; in 1978, nearly half of all married women are so employed. The relationship of women's labor force participation to childbearing and childrearing is changing in complex ways. Forty-one percent of all mothers with children under the age of six are in the labor force. Nearly half of all mothers with children under 18 are in the labor force (Odendahl & Smith, 1978).

The papers of Beckman and of Thornton and Camburn take independent looks at the multivariate relationships among sex role and fertility variables for women who seek to combine home and work roles. These studies illustrate some of the conceptual and methodological sophistication that will be needed to investigate causality of such relationships. At the same time, they also illustrate the limitations of multivariate techniques that rely on assumptions of linearity and unidirectional relationships.

Beckman makes an important conceptual distinction between attitudes and behavior in her study and underscores the need to separate analyses by ethnic group. The motherhood mandate reflects the norms of the majority group in our society, but the context of motherhood is very different for minority women.

Beckman reports a number of significant complex relationships between sex role behaviors within and outside of the family, but the low correlations lead her to conclude that the interrelationships are subtle. Such subtlety demands refinement in our definitions of sex role. As Hare-Mustin notes, changing role requirements of motherhood per se are only recently receiving systematic study. The development of procedures to study motherhood rather than mothers is an important direction for research.

Thornton and Camburn point to the power of perceived role definitions on childbearing variables. They report that what they describe as "home orientation" plays a "central and vital role in defining women's status and place" (p. 79). A closer look at the nature of home orientation reveals that it basically involves beliefs about the impact of a mother's working on her children's development, her relationship with her children, her happiness if she devotes herself to her children, and her guilt if she does not. An explicit conceptual distinction between motherhood role expectations and other family-related responsibilities is needed in further research. The quantification of the direct, indirect, and reciprocal mechanisms by which beliefs about motherhood relate to women's exercise of options are a major challenge to our methods.

Allison's study of role conflict of women in infertile couples provides yet another dimension to this challenge. Her work is a cogent reminder that understanding interrelationships among sex role and fertility variables will require more than complex multivariate statistical approaches. Conceptual models that integrate biological, psychological, social, and structural levels of analyses must be developed.

Future research can build on the work of Beckman, Thornton and Camburn, and Allison by making conceptual distinctions between perceived prescriptions and proscriptions of the motherhood role, and the perceived incompatibility of these prescriptions and proscriptions with those of other sex roles (e.g., that of wife) for women of different ethnic groups. Such distinctions might explain some of the unexpected correlations between traditional attitudes and behaviors and fertility variables found in these studies. Correlations between sex role and fertility variables will continue to be problematical, however, as long as women are not able to attain reproductive freedom.

## Reproductive Freedom

Kearney describes how changes in laws, policies and education that enable women to control their reproduction continue to meet intense resistance and controversy. Nonetheless, in 1976, 1 in 12 marital births was unwanted by the parents at the time of conception, compared with 1 in 5 just a decade ago (Planned Parenthood, 1977). Despite such progress, 250,000–300,000 married women in the U.S. each year still have unwanted births. A disproportionate number are low and marginal income women (Munson, 1977). The subsequent physical, psychological, social, and economic consequences continue to provide major barriers to the improvement of women's status, impeding women's ability to take advantage of other reforms.

Kearney points out that abortion's role in controlling reproduction is greater for vulnerable groups. In 1975, 3/4 of the one million women having abortions were unmarried; 1/3 of them were teenagers. The abortion rate for nonwhite women is at least double that for whites in every age category (Tietze, 1977).

Denying public funds for abortion has its most direct impact on the reproductive freedom of poor mothers, since they are least able to afford abortions otherwise. The average abortion cost is $280—an expensive item considering the average monthly welfare payment for a family is $238 (Lincoln, Doring-Bradley, Lindheim, & Cotterill, 1977).

Unwanted childbearing has been linked with poverty, child abuse and filicide, juvenile delinquency, marital disruption, and a variety of other psychological, social, and economic ills (Terhune, 1974). Evidence suggests that individuals may overestimate their ability to adapt to a new infant (especially the first-born), but the reverse does not appear to be true. Data from the methodologically sophisticated Hawaii Pregnancy, Birth Control, and Abortion Study suggest that women decide to terminate their pregnancies based on an evaluation of objective factors related to each woman's capacity to care for the child (Steinhoff, Smith, & Diamond, 1972).

The methodological problems of studies of unwanted pregnancy and childbearing are a major source of frustration to researchers. However, it does appear that if a woman requests an abortion, to deny her the service means to force her to bear an offspring that is at higher risk for a variety of physical, psychological, social, and economic problems (Forssman & Thuwe, 1966; Dytrych, Matejcek, Schuller, David, & Friedman, 1977). In contrast, the few methodologically sound studies of legalized abortion "on request" suggest that the psychological implications of such abortions are mostly benign (Schusterman, 1977).

Research on controversies surrounding abortion and unwanted childbearing reflects the current context of imperfect contraception. Advances in reproductive technology might eliminate these controversies. However, Fidell, Hoffman, and Keith-Spiegel's study of the implications of the ability to select the sex of one's offspring reminds us that such advances have other social implications. It also underscores the need for feminist evaluation of technological advances in reproductive control.

Those authors conclude that the use of sex-choice techniques given current preferences for male first-borns may, on balance, be detrimental to the status of women by strengthening the sex-typing of both sexes. They also report that respondents who approve of the goals of the women's movement are more likely than those who disapprove of those goals to desire a female first-born child. Since women in that group were also more likely to say they did not want any children, the authors suggest that one strategy for minimizing the detrimental impact of sex-choice techniques might be to foster pro-natalism among feminists.

This suggestion raises a number of issues, the most obvious being the potential conflict between feminist and population concerns. More important here is the illustration of the potential of the motherhood mandate to influence feminist thought. Women have traditionally been encouraged to overlook their personal needs and circumstances and have children for the good of a variety of people, including "only" children, grandparents, and husbands. Adding "other women" to this list does not recognize the pervasive and devastating consequences of the motherhood mandate for women. It also does not recognize the implications of the ability to opt for voluntary childlessness for the definition of motherhood.

## Voluntary Childlessness

Houseknecht's research documents the need to look at the interactions between personality characteristics and environmental supports for the childless decision over the life cycle. The voluntary childless decision is a phenomenon deserving of study in its own right. But, as Kearney notes, the apparent increase in voluntary childlessness since 1960 and the organization of an advocacy group for child-free couples, the National Organization for Non-Parents (NON), signal profound changes for the meaning of motherhood that deserve attention as well.

There is overwhelming scientific evidence that we value what we perceive ourselves to have freely chosen (Worchel & Cooper, 1976). Insofar as voluntary childlessness is considered a valued option for women in our society, motherhood itself becomes an option rather than a mandate. Perceiving oneself to have chosen a motherhood *option* should result in an increased commitment to that choice. Investigating the impact of that commitment must be included in priorities for research on parenting and other family relationships, particularly research on the mother-child relationship.

The implications of a context having voluntary childlessness as a legitimate option go beyond an impact on the family unit. Since the motherhood mandate pervades our institutions (e.g., insurance and tax systems), the widespread assumption that women can and will legitimately opt for voluntary childlessness would force a reexamination and restructuring of those institutions. Some of this examination is beginning to occur (Peck & Senderowitz, 1974). For example, NON has a project that is aimed toward sensitizing publishers, educators, and teachers to pronatalist bias in textbooks.

In discussing the impact of the ability to choose to remain childless, the actuality of that ability for women must be considered. We have seen that the ability to control reproduction is not equally accessible to all women in our society. Advances in contraceptive technology have made it all too easy to assume reproductive freedom as a given, with research on voluntary childlessness proceeding from that premise. The issues of voluntary childlessness thus become those of mature middle class women who have sufficient experience and resources to control their fertility. The choice is denied to other segments of our society, particularly the poor and the young. This not only limits the ability of women in those groups to choose the option of childlessness—it means that they are denied the potential benefit of *choosing* to have children. Motherhood in this context has a very different meaning for those groups.

Houseknecht's research on voluntary childlessness points to the importance of autonomy and achievement orientation in women exercising that option. Whether or not some women arrived at the decision to remain childless through a series of postponements after marriage or via an early decision before marriage, they were equally characterized by these attributes. Thornton and Camburn report an association between a women's orientation towards planning and her unwanted childbearing. These very different studies illustrate how the ability to control one's reproduction is not derived solely from technological means.

Freeman's (1977) research on abortion dramatically illustrates the effects of not teaching women to plan and value their lives on their ability to control their reproduction. Most women in her sample were faced with unwanted pregnancies because they had not seen themselves as instrumental in planning pregnancy. As Freeman describes it "pregnancy happened to them. . . . Their experiences had trained them to be receptive, to value themselves in terms of other's responses more than through their own contributions. They had no history of feeling what they did made any difference, that their own actions and decisions had value to themselves and others" (Freeman, p. 510).

Unwanted pregnancy can be considered a direct reflection of

women's disadvantaged status. Little girls are socialized to have low self-esteem, high need for approval and aspirations limited to motherhood. We have taught little boys to denigrate little girls, to separate sex from affection and to exploit the opposite sex through "conquest" (Russo & Brackbill, 1973; Scales, 1977). These are not characteristics that provide a foundation for responsible sexual behavior on the part of either sex, young or old.

Reproductive freedom also comes from the ability to say "no" to males who would ask that a woman engage in unprotected intercourse counter to her self-interest; it involves having goals and aspirations that make planning one's life (and avoiding unwanted pregnancy) meaningful; it involves developing a sense of competence and independence in women so that if they do develop an intimate relationship they will have the knowledge and ability to minimize the risk of unwanted pregnancy.

Relationships between sex roles and fertility are thus indeed complex, even when one limits the analyses to the U.S. The articles assembled here only highlight some of the dimensions of this complexity. They document the importance of developing models that integrate biological, psychological, social, and structural variables. They demonstrate the importance of context, the changing character of which demands special attention to ethnic group differences as well as cohort and time-of-measurement effects. They show the need to take an interactionist perspective that recognizes continuous socialization throughout the life cycle.

## TOWARDS AN INTERACTIONIST PERSPECTIVE

The development of an interactionist perspective in our research requires more than the computer technology and the statistical techniques to analyze multivariate interaction effects. It requires the development of theoretical formulations that explicate mechanisms of interaction and the research designs to test them. Such formulations will require going beyond the question of how *much* variance in behavior our studies can explain to the question of *how* the variance is produced. To advance our knowledge we thus must seek to study *metavariance* of behavior, i.e., to study the variance of the variance (Russo, 1972; 1979). Switching the perspective of our models from means to variances will hopefully lay the foundation for a focus on process. Achieving such a focus is perhaps the greatest challenge facing researchers who seek to understand the psychology of women.

# REFERENCES

Bernard, J. *The future of motherhood.* New York: Dial Press, 1974.

Dytrych, Z., Matejcek, Z., Schuller, V., David, H. P., & Friedman, H. Children born to women denied abortion. *Family Planning Perspectives,* 1975, *7,* 165–171.

Fein, R. Research on fathering: Social policy and an emergent perspective. *Journal of Social Issues,* 1978, *34,* 122–135.

Forssman, H., & Thuwe, I. One-hundred and twenty children born after application for therapeutic abortion refused. *Acta Psychiatrica Scandinavica,* 1966, *42,* 71–88.

Freeman, E. Influence of personality attributes on abortion experiences. *American Journal of Orthopsychiatry,* 1977, *47,* 503–513.

Hollingworth, L. Social devices for compelling women to bear and rear children. *American Journal of Sociology,* 1916, *22,* 19–29.

Lincoln, R., Doring-Bradley, B., Lindheim, B. L., & Cotterill, M. A. The court, the congress and the president: Turning back the clock on the pregnant poor. *Family Planning Perspectives,* 1977, *9,* 207–214.

Munson, M. Wanted and unwanted births reported by mothers 15–44 years of age: United States, 1973, *Advance data from vital & health statistics of the National Center for Health Statistics,* August 10, 1977, No. 9.

Odendahl, T., & Smith, L. Women's employment, *Comment,* 1978, *11,* 1–2.

Peck, E., & Senderowitz, J. (Eds.). *Pronatalism: The myth of mom and apple pie.* New York: Thomas Y. Crowell Co., 1974.

Planned Parenthood. *Planned births, the future of the family and the quality of American life.* New York: The Alan Guttmacher Institute, 1977.

Russo, N. F. Some observations on the role of personality variables in fertility research. *Conference proceedings: Psychological measurement in the study of population problems.* Institute for Personality Assessment and Research, University of California, Berkeley, 1972, 62–68.

Russo, N. F. Beyond adolescence: Suggested directions for studying female development in the middle and later years. In F. Denmark & J. Sherman (Eds.), *New Directions in research on the psychology of women.* New York: Psychological Dimensions, 1979.

Russo, N. F. The motherhood mandate. *Journal of Social Issues,* 1976, *32,* 143–154.

Russo, N. F., & Brackbill, Y. Population and youth. In J. Fawcett (Ed.), *Psychological perspectives on population.* New York: Basic Books, 1973.

Scales, P. Males and morals: Teenage contraceptive behavior amid the double standard. *The Family Coordinator,* July 1977, 211–222.

Shusterman, L. The psychosocial factors of the abortion experience: A critical review. *Psychology of Women Quarterly,* 1976, *1,* 79–106.

Steinhoff, P., Smith, R., & Diamond, M. The Hawaii pregnancy, birth control, and abortion study: Social psychological aspects. *Conference proceedings: Psychological measurement in the study of population problems.* Institute of Personality Assessment and Research, University of California, Berkeley, 1972, 33–40.

Terhune, K. *A review of the actual and expected consequences of family size.* Calspan report no. DP-5333-6-1, July 31, 1974.

Tietze, C. Induced Abortion: 1977 Supplement, *Reports of population/family planning,* 1977, *14,* 1–20.

Worchel, S., & Cooper, J. *Understanding social psychology.* Homewood, Ill.: Dorsey Press, 1976.

# Feminist Challenges to the Social Structure and Sex Roles

Helen R. Kearney

*Annandale, Virginia*

A social-psychological and historical context for understanding contemporary sex roles, fertility, parenting, and the family is provided by reviewing origins and objectives of the Women's Movement. Feminist efforts to change social structures affecting women's choice of roles and fertility require continued attention. Increased voluntary childlessness seriously challenges the concept of motherhood as central to adult feminine identity and legitimization of choice in whether or not to become a parent provides a new context for studying women, sex roles, fertility, and their complex relationships to the social structure. Continued challenges to premises, methodologies, and conclusions of such research are urged.

The Women's Movement has provided feminist challenges to common assumptions about the "proper" role of women. Legislative conflicts associated with feminist efforts to change the social structure have included such areas as suffrage, the Equal Rights Amendment to the United States Constitution, employment rights, property rights, child care, maternity benefits, and the means to control reproduction (Freeman, 1975; Sherif, 1976, pp. 361–392; WEAL, 1977). Only since the 1960s, however, has the centrality of motherhood to adult feminine identity been seriously challenged (Russo, 1976). The grow-

---

The author gratefully acknowledges the contributions of Barbara Moely, Department of Psychology, Newcomb College, Tulane University, and Jane Weiss, Department of Sociology, University of Iowa. This paper was developed while the author was working as an Assistant Professor in the Department of Psychology at Tulane. An earlier version was presented during a workshop led by the author with the following invited resource persons: Charles R. Figley (Purdue University), Virginia Hayes Sibbison (Welfare Research, Inc.), and Heather Weiss (Harvard University), at the Groves Conference on Marriage and the Family, Grossinger, New York, May 5, 1977. The theme of the conference was "Quality Parenting: How to Achieve It." Direct reprint requests to: 3358 Woodburn Road, #31, Annandale, Virginia 22003.

*Psychology of Women Quarterly, Vol. 4(1) Fall 1979*
0361-6843/79/1500-0016$00.95 © 1979 Human Sciences Press

ing phenomenon of individuals and couples voluntarily choosing to remain childless provides quite a new context for studying the relationship between male and female roles and fertility. This different context challenges the motherhood mandate (i.e., the assumption that all women should bear and raise children), and requires a reexamination of the premises underlying research.

The contemporary Women's Movement is the second wave of a social movement originating in 1848 at Seneca Falls, New York, when Lucretia Mott and Elizabeth Cady Stanton organized the first Women's Rights Convention, which issued a Declaration of Sentiments (modeled on the Declaration of Independence), and demanded the right to vote. When that right was finally attained in 1920, the almost 80 years of lobbying, traveling, speaking, and writing had taken their toll on proponents' energies. The first wave of the Women's Movement entered a quiescent phase (Flexner, 1959; O'Neill, 1969; Stanton, 1971).

A combination of factors during the early 1960s resulted in the development of a motivational base for the contemporary Women's Movement. In 1961, President John Kennedy, encouraged by the Director of the U.S. Women's Bureau, Esther Peterson, established a Presidential Commission on the Status of Women. The Commission's publication, *American Women* (1963), documented rights and opportunities routinely denied to women of the United States. By 1967, commissions on the status of women had been established in all 50 states (Freeman, 1975; Hole & Levine, 1971; Sherif, 1976). The first federal acts prohibiting discrimination based on sex were the Equal Pay Act, 1963; Title VII of the 1964 Civil Rights Act prohibiting sex discrimination in employment; and Executive Order 11246, 1965, as amended by Executive Order 11375, 1967, the latter prohibiting sex discrimination in employment by federal contractors and subcontractors. According to Freeman (1975), these events created a "climate of expectation" that something would be done to correct legal and economic injustices, a crucial step in the formation of a social movement (Toch, 1965). But focusing only on work proved to be too narrow a perspective.

Publication of *The Feminine Mystique* (Friedan, 1963) stirred millions of women by its identification of "the problem that has no name" and the theme, "I want something more than my husband and my children and my home." The author soon became a key figure in organizing the second wave of the Women's Movement by focusing these sentiments on needed changes in the structure of contemporary society.

## NATIONAL ORGANIZATION FOR WOMEN

By 1966, it became apparent to Friedan and others that the Equal Employment Opportunity Commission was not adequately enforcing the provisions against sex discrimination in Title VII of the 1964 Civil Rights Act. As a result, Friedan organized the National Organization for Women (NOW); chapters proliferated across the nation. Composed of both men and women, NOW's membership grew from 300 in 1966 to 80,000 in 1978 (Sherif, 1976, p. 375; Smeal, 1978). Today, as the largest feminist organization whose specific objectives are to obtain civil rights and equality for women, the NOW Bill of Rights (adopted at its first national conference in 1967) provides an index to the priorities of the Women's Movement. The demands included:

(1) Equal Rights Constitutional Amendment;
(2) enforce laws banning sex discrimination in employment;
(3) maternity leave rights in employment and in social security benefits;
(4) tax deduction for home and child care expenses for working parents;
(5) child day care centers;
(6) equal and unsegregated education;
(7) equal job training opportunities and allowances for women in poverty; and
(8) the right of women to control their reproductive lives (Morgan, 1970, p. 512).

## WOMEN'S LIBERATION

During 1967–1968, events in the lives of women who had been involved in the anti-war, student, and black civil rights movements resulted in the development of feminist groups in five different cities (Chicago, Toronto, Seattle, Detroit, and Gainesville, Florida) (Freeman, 1975, p. 59). According to Freeman (1975, pp. 57–58), the "idea" of women's "liberation" was first raised at a Students for a Democratic Society (SDS) convention in 1965, but male radicals ridiculed the notion. Subsequent "rap" groups of women, convening without the radical men, came to be known as "consciousness-raising" or "women's liberation" groups, and formed rapidly and autonomously across the nation. Their shared examination of member's "personal" problems revealed previously unrecognized commonalities, resulting in reformulation of these problems in sociopolitical terms. By 1967, SDS passed a resolution calling for full participation of women in that organization and the women suggested that SDS work for the following goals:

(1) communal child care;
(2) wide dissemination of contraceptives;
(3) easily available abortions; and
(4) equal sharing of housework (Freeman, 1975, p. 58).

These two sets of demands (from NOW and Women's Liberation) generated in quite different settings and age groups, overlap remarkably.

By 1974, two additional demands were included in NOW's Bill of Rights: equal access to public accommodations and housing; and partnership marriages of equalized rights and shared responsibilities (NOW, 1974). It is important to note that early feminist objectives addressed needed social structural changes, and, except for the shared housework demand, did not emphasize change in sex roles on an interpersonal level.

The pervasiveness of parenting issues in these lists is striking and reflects the traditional concept of the centrality of motherhood to womanhood. A woman's ability to control her own reproductive life gives her the power to define her own adult feminine identity. At this point, the cliché of the movement, "the personal is the political," becomes apt. A woman's ability to define herself intersects with society's laws regulating expression of sexuality, access to information and services for sex education, contraception, abortion, and sterilization, and access to educational and employment opportunities that permit alternatives to motherhood. O'Neill, an historian, has pointed out that it is all too easy to fail to appreciate the limits that the organization of society places upon the larger aspirations of women (Sherif, 1976). Since such laws are based on the premise that adult womanhood equates with motherhood, a woman's ability to control her own self-definition and achieve alternative aspirations, becomes dependent upon political action. Increased political involvement by feminists has contributed to institutional changes that have a direct impact on the relationship between sex roles and fertility.

## CONTROL OF ONE'S OWN REPRODUCTION

### Laws, Policies, and Education

Women have long sought control over their own reproduction as a means of protecting their health and the quality of their parenting.

With the exception of the post-World War II years (1950s), the birth rate in the U.S. (aided by recent advances in contraceptive technology) has been steadily declining since the 1800s, from an average of seven children per woman to approximately two per woman (Baer & Bush, 1974). Many individuals and organizations concerned with population growth have formed coalitions with groups in the Women's Movement to strive for changes in laws and medical practices which will facilitate reproductive control. The Presidential Commission on Population Growth and the American Future provided a strong institutional mandate for voluntary control and stabilization of population growth (Rockefeller, 1972, p. 4). Such collaborative efforts have been responsible for changing laws and policies in most states regarding availability of contraceptive information and services.

There has been limited progress in developing family life and sex education courses in school systems. Few consider alternatives to parenthood, reflecting a "pronatalist indoctrination" (Russo, 1972, p. 361). In 1976, the American School Health Association reported that 28 states and the District of Columbia either require, or identify as a local option, "comprehensive" health education in the public schools. Only six states and the District require some form of "family life" or "sex education." Few teach about birth control methods, and one, Louisiana, specifically forbids contraceptive education (Ambrose, 1976, p. 78; 1978, p. 8). Yet, more than one million teenagers in the U.S. become pregnant annually (Jaffe & Dryfoos, 1976, p. 167).

Assumptions about motherhood have seriously hindered policy development and health planning. Consider the proposed DHEW regulations for "National Guidelines for Health Planning" issued late in 1977. The guidelines only use child deliveries as the measure of fertility-related services to a community and on this basis will close underutilized hospital facilities, notably obstetrical units. Failure to include infertility treatment, sterilization, and abortion services grossly underestimates the demand for services and, according to the Planned Parenthood Federation, the omissions result in "insufficient and inadequate criteria for the planning and effective utilization of obstetrical units . . ." (Rosoff, 1978a, p. 5). Voluntary surgical sterilization is now the most popular method of fertility regulation and increasing requests for it are likely (Gonzales & Ruben, 1978, p. 3).

## Legalized Abortion

Reproductive control is the most crucial arena for affecting women's ability for self-definition, and as long as there is no perfect contraceptive, access to legal abortion is essential for such control. Prior to 1970, relatively few women could obtain legal abortions in the U.S. Such medical treatment was particularly inaccessible for minority group members. In a 20-year review of maternal deaths made by Gold and his colleagues in 1965 in New York City, it was estimated that one in four puerperal deaths among whites and one in two among nonwhites and Puerto Ricans were due to illegal abortions (Callahan, 1970, pp. 133-136).

Years of lobbying, rallies, mass public speak-outs on abortion, and landmark court cases eventuated in a U.S. Supreme Court decision in January, 1973, declaring most state laws regulating abortion to be unconstitutional on the grounds of invasion of privacy of the woman. The *Roe* v. *Wade* decision indicated that states cannot regulate physician and patient decisions concerning abortion during the first trimester of pregnancy at all, and during the second trimester only to the extent necessary to protect maternal health (Local Regulations, 1978, pp. 1-2).

The important role that abortion plays in fertility control is reflected in the frequency of its use. Tietze estimated that 2.3-2.5 million abortions were performed in the U.S. during 1972-1974 (1977a, p. 12). During that period, mortality rates associated with pregnancy and childbirth ranged from 11.1 per 100,000 (ages 15-19 years) to 71.4 per 100,000 (ages 40-44 years), reflecting greater health risks than legal abortions for comparable age groups (1.2 per 100,000 and 1.8 per 100,000) (Tietze, 1977b, p. 74). Clearly, massive numbers of women annually seek to terminate unwanted pregnancies, and legal access to such services protects their health.

Despite the availability of such medical and demographic evidence, and the U.S. Supreme Court decision, the U.S. House passed the Hyde Amendment to the Department of Labor and Department of Health, Education, and Welfare (DHEW) appropriations bill in 1977. Thus, expenditure of federal Medicaid funds was prohibited for abortions except when the woman's life is endangered, or in cases of reported rape or incest, or when two physicians certify severe health damage would result if the woman carried the pregnancy to term (Rosoff, 1977, p. 1). In addition, in 1977, over 40 constitutional amendments were introduced to ban legal abortions in the 95th Congress. Some of the proposed amendments would prohibit *all* abortions, even when a woman's life is at stake (Mulhauser, 1978). The assumption that women are for having babies appears to override considerations of rape, incest, health risks, or even the woman's life for some legislators.

In 1978, DHEW Secretary Joseph A. Califano, Jr., a known opponent of Medicaid-funded abortions, issued final regulations implementing the Hyde amendment, and waived normal procedures for publishing proposed regulations. In the process, he ignored the petition of 24 national health, civil rights, religious, and feminist organizations for public hearings on the regulations, illustrating the power of even non-elected members of the bureaucracy to impose the motherhood mandate (Rosoff, 1978b, p. 1).

The U.S. Supreme Court ruled in 1977 that states are not required to share the cost of Medicaid abortions with the federal government (Congress Ends, 1978, p. 5). By 1978, less than a third of the states were reimbursing health providers for Medicaid abortion costs; the others paid only when the woman's life was threatened, except Arizona, which does not have a Medicaid program (Rosoff, 1978a, p. 4). The strength of the motherhood mandate becomes more apparent when one considers the Medicaid decisions in the context of the demand for sound fiscal policy. Based on a formula (developed by P. Cutright and F. S. Jaffe) to assess the short-term costs and benefits of fertility control programs, the following has been estimated:

> If one-third of Medicaid women desiring an abortion give birth in the absence of public funding for abortion, the first-year public costs would be $200 million. If a higher proportion of these women are forced to go to term, this figure will increase correspondingly. In addition, the first-year costs do not reflect the increased social welfare expenditures that will be needed for at last some of these families for many years to come (Lincoln, Döring-Bradley, Lindheim, & Cotterill, 1977, p. 213).

Since 1973, 13 of the required 34 states have asked Congress to convene a constitutional convention for the purpose of proposing a new amendment to the U.S. Constitution, which would define the fetus from the moment of fertilization as a person guaranteed a "right to life," thus prohibiting all abortions (Donovan, 1978, p. 62). Across the nation, in the past year, increasing numbers of "sit-ins," acts of violence, arson, and property damage against patients, personnel, and centers offering problem pregnancy and abortion services have been noted (Harold, 1978, pp. 1–2).

The strategy of opponents of abortion and the right of a woman to control her own reproductive life is multi-faceted, involving structural, social, and psychological tactics. To understand the constraints that influence the relationship between sex roles and fertility, they must be analyzed at the legislative, executive, and judicial branches of the federal government, as well as at the state, local government, and private citizen levels of action. Analyses and up-to-date summaries of state laws and policies, federal legislative actions, and court decisions dealing with family planning, birth control, abortion, and sterilization are available in *Family Planning/Population Reporter,* and *Planned Parenthood/World Population Washington Memo,* from the Alan Guttmacher Institute and the *NARAL Newsletter* from the National Abortion Rights Action League in Washington, D.C.

The controversy over legalized abortion has been a lively one for more than a decade. Many analysts thought that legitimization of choice in whether or not to terminate a pregnancy was successfully achieved when the U.S. Supreme Court made its decision in 1973. More careful scrutiny of the issues reveals that efforts to erode or eliminate the freedom of choice remain a continuous threat, and are most effective when directed toward vulnerable groups, the young and the poor (Local Regulations, 1978, pp. 1–2). People familiar with the abortion controversy in state legislatures during the 1960s will have a sense of déjà vu at the repetition of tactics (bureaucratic delays, cumbersome credentialing and licensing procedures, conflicts over arbitrary time limits, and definitions of permissible conditions for termination, e.g., rape, incest, fetal conditions) that are being re-enacted in both the halls of Congress and the state legislatures as debate on public funding for abortions continues (Callahan, 1970, pp. 202–204; Cisler, 1970).

## VOLUNTARY CHILDLESSNESS

A serious challenge to the motherhood mandate is posed for the first time by the growing numbers of men and women since 1960 who chose to remain single and/or to postpone marriage and family formation (Russo, 1976; Stein, 1976, p. 14). In 1976, the U.S. Bureau of the Census indicated that there were nearly three times as many wives under 30 expecting to remain childless in 1975 (4.6%) as in 1964 (1.7%) (Silka & Kiesler, 1977, p. 24). Determined childless couples use the pill and sterilization, rejecting less effective birth control methods. Situational factors contributing to the choice to remain childless include the degree of success the couple is experiencing in employment or career development, peer group support (Houseknecht, 1977), and stability in the marriage. In Silka and Kiesler's (1977) study of 61 childless couples, career and income considerations were perceived as the most important factors bearing on possible changes in their intentions to remain childless. They emphasized that "since wives are more likely to make the final decision, their job status possibilities will be crucial" (p. 24). In addition, they recognized the influence of the state of the mid- to upper-level job market on the fertility of such couples. Other authors have also pointed out the crucial importance of meaningful alternatives to motherhood in the form of more than "dead-end" jobs if continued low fertility is to be maintained, and positive mental health encouraged (Blake, 1969; Chesler, 1972; Witt, 1976; Baer & Bush, 1974). Voluntary childlessness compels us to alter the way we think about sex roles, forcing reexamination of premises of our research.

## SOCIAL SCIENCE RESEARCH: A RE-EXAMINATION

Feminists have been highly critical of theoretical and research efforts by social scientists regarding women, sex roles, and parenting (Baer & Sherif, 1974; Bart, 1971a & b; Bernard, 1974; Pleck & Sawyer, 1974; Rossi, 1968 & 1971; Shields, 1975; Sherif, 1976; Sherman, 1971; Weisstein, 1970). Many have noted that research on male subjects dominates the psychological literature, and that there is a greater tendency to generalize to all human beings when males have been studied than when females have served as subjects. Failure to identify the sex of the subjects is not uncommon.

Weisstein (1970) urged a refocusing of psychological research toward studying human behavior in its social context with particular attention paid to expectations stemming from "authorities," rather than limiting research to traditional intrapsychic phenomena. Sherif (1976) has emphasized that social stereotypes of men and women in the U. S. "describe a *role relationship* in which the behaviors described (true or not) cannot occur independently of another person" (p. 297). "Trait" theories of personality end up making attributions to individuals based on behaviors that can occur only during interaction in human relationships (Sherif, 1976, p. 297). To understand human behavior, one must examine the social context and availability of alternatives, and the relationship *between* men and women, paying particular attention to the power dimension (which more often than not, encourages or requires dependency on males by females).

Shields (1975) provided an historical context from which to judge the role of social myths and their use as justifications of the existing social system. By tracing the study of three topics during the functionalist era in psychology (structural sex differences in brains, the hypothesis of greater male variability and its relations to social and educational issues, and "maternal instinct"), Shields cleverly demonstrated "that science played handmaiden to social myths . . ." (p. 753).

The growing phenomenon of voluntary childlessness has helped us to see that the assumption of a "maternal instinct" probably indicates more about researchers' biases, sex role stereotyping, expectations of fertility, and lack of alternatives in a pronatalist societal context than it does about female psychology. Baer and Sherif (1974) noted that such challenges may require abandonment or revision of biased assumptions, but should result in strengthening the fundamental premises of the chosen field of inquiry by forcing reexamination of the research literature, redefinition of the problems, and stimulation of new research. We must examine conclusions and methodology, and reach an understanding of which questions have been taboo, and why. In doing so, considering the level of analysis appropriate to solution of the problem is crucial.

Kanter's (1976) discussion of occupational segregation of the sexes and three models for change is instructive. Her models roughly correspond to individual, role, and organizational levels of analysis of social interaction and have different implications (due to the level of analysis utilized) regarding assumptions made about women and men, the appropriate level of intervention, scope of change, likely effectiveness, and potential for backlash. Focusing on the individual permits the organizational structure to remain intact, and continues sex role stereotyping, reinforcing traditional attitudes by people in power (usually men). Focus on role relationships and division of labor in the family as the key to understanding occupational segregation of women into inferior positions in the labor force tends to generate an image of women as overcommitted and struggling with role conflicts when they take on extra-familial work roles without relinquishing some home responsibilities to their partners, or to institutional innovations. Such a strategy does little to benefit women in the work force not encumbered by familial commitments, nor does it differentiate sufficiently between types of work situations and family situations which generate role strains based on their interaction.

The "social structural" model, in Kanter's opinion, has greater potential for reducing occupational segregation, thus providing more flexibility in selection of adult roles, either as worker, parent, nonparent, or some combination. Research and intervention at this level have been minimal. Stewart and Winter (1977), and Jane Weiss and her colleagues are notable exceptions with their cross-national analyses of female participation in occupational systems, legal status, and political incorporation of women (Ramirez & Weiss, 1976; Ramirez, Weiss, & Tracy, 1975; Weiss, Ramirez, & Tracy, 1975). This third model makes fewer assumptions about roles between the sexes, thus reducing the likelihood of stereotyping. Focus on time patterns, opportunity structures, communication patterns, dominance structures, and sex ratios within and across hierarchical levels helps us to understand that as women gain power in work situations, roles within the family are affected. Thus, the organizational level of analysis permits recognition of the reciprocal relationship between the larger social system and the family, avoiding the unidirectional limitations of the second "role related" model. Cross-cultural comparisons help in avoiding ethnocentric conclusions.

Fallacious assumptions about motherhood, sex roles, situational determinants, and causality have served to influence research on parenting over the years. Freudian theory guided most research on early personality development during the 1930s and 1940s, focusing on the mother-child relationship and interpreting "inadequate mothering" as a major factor leading to emotional disturbances (Ribble, 1943; Spitz, 1945). An assumption of unidirectional causality (from the mother to the child) was characteristic.

Critical reviews of these early studies noted their methodological inadequacies and inconclusive findings. Subsequent research during the 1950s and 1960s on animals and humans indicated that many different conditions were included in the term "maternal deprivation." Uncritical acceptance of the term interfered with understanding the situational determinants of a variety of developmental consequences (Yarrow, Rubenstein, & Pedersen, 1975, p. 4). Such biased interpretations reflected the tendency to focus on intrapsychic phenomena (Weisstein, 1970), the power of the motherhood mandate (Russo, 1976), and "science playing handmaiden to social myths" (Shields, 1975).

Over the years, various theoretical approaches, and more complexity have been introduced in research design, and targets for scrutiny have broadened to include the father, siblings, other adults, peers, other models (e.g., television characters), examination of reciprocal interaction effects, and social norms (Ainsworth, 1973; Bandura & Walters, 1963; Bell, 1968; Berlyne, 1960; Ervin-Tripp, 1973; Hartup, 1970; Hebb, 1949; Hetherington, 1965; Hunt, 1964; Inhelder, 1969; Kohlberg, 1966; Martin, 1975; Parsons & Bales, 1955; Piaget, 1953; Sherif & Sherif, 1964; Sinclair-de-Zwart, 1969). Bronfenbrenner (1977) has emphasized that growing attention must be paid to situational determinants of behavior, the ecological setting, and cross-cultural comparisons. Other factors which have influenced the character of developmental research have been increasingly sophisticated observational schemes and laboratory procedures for data collection from infancy onward (Moely, 1977), rapid technological improvements in computers' abilities to handle large quantities of data, and more sophisticated statistical procedures (Parke, 1977).

These changes in developmental theory and research have been occurring simultaneously with the growth of the Women's Movement. Feminists have contributed their share of critical commentary on sexism in family studies, providing vivid examples of the ways sexism shapes which topics are viewed as legitimate for research (Bart, 1971a & b). For example, Bart described Alice Rossi's (1968) critique of Parson's sex-based distinction between expressive and instrumental roles in the family. Rossi emphasized that to be functional as parents, males and females must have *both* expressive and instrumental dimensions in their roles, and that assuming such sex-based differences restricts theory building in family sociology (Bart, 1971b, p. 738). Such critiques, combined with new journal policies concerning sex as a variable, have served to heighten awareness that reporting sex differences/similarities is a relevant endeavor (Etaugh & Spandikow, 1977).

Contemporary research appears to be concentrating on many positive features of parenthood, effects of alternative child care arrangements, and ways of enhancing children's cognitive-motivational development. This research seems to reflect greater respect for parents, and, with growing numbers of women in the labor force, an appreciation for flexibility in parental roles (Etaugh, 1974, p. 90; Kreps & Clark, 1975; Maccoby & Feldman, 1972; Rheingold, 1973; White, 1975; Yarrow, et al., 1975; Heber, Garber, Harrington, Hoffman & Falender, 1972; Lamb, 1977a & b). Such research will continue to require the critical eye of feminist scholars and a cognizance of the effects of social structure.

## CONCLUSIONS

A social-psychological and historical context for reassessment of our understanding of contemporary sex roles, fertility, parenting, and the family was provided by reviewing feminists' objectives for social change. The original demands from the Women's Movement focused primarily on needed social structural changes and did not emphasize change in sex roles on an interpersonal level. However, feminist goals are integrally related to the freedom to choose whether or not to become a parent, the definition of quality of parenting, the nature of sex roles in our society, and *options* for achieving a meaningful life.

Examination of laws, policies, and educational issues affecting reproductive control and controversy concerning the Hyde amendment and public funding of abortions heightens awareness that the goal of reproductive control for all women, rich and poor alike, is not yet a reality. The strategy and tactics used by those opposing a woman's right to control her own reproductive life reveal the pervasiveness of the motherhood mandate and pronatalist societal structure. Complex analyses are necessary to understand their full impact on women's lives and our perceptions of sex roles and fertility.

The growing trend of voluntary childlessness challenges the concept of the centrality of motherhood to womanhood and illustrates important situational determinants affecting choices about parenthood. The significance of access to more than "dead-end" jobs for encouraging positive mental health and continued low fertility is emphasized.

Feminists' critiques of theoretical and research efforts on women, sex roles, and parenting question basic assumptions in many academic disciplines. Heeding the level of analysis of social interaction is crucial for understanding possibilities for individual and social change, and types of interventions likely to attain desired social goals. Continued challenges to our premises, methodologies, and conclusions serve constructively to improve social science research. The lively debate over these issues makes the area a particularly exciting one for renewed research efforts tempered by increased sensitivity to the complex relationships between sex roles, fertility, parenting, the family, and the social structure.

## REFERENCES

Ainsworth, M. D. S. The development of infant-mother attachment. In B. M. Caldwell & H. N. Ricciuti (Eds.), *Review of child development research.* Vol. 3. Chicago: University of Chicago Press, 1973.

Ambrose, L. Birth control education in Michigan's schools: Elements of a successful 10-year effort. *Family Planning/Population Reporter,* 1978, 7(1), 8–10.

Ambrose, L. Sex education in the public schools: The need for official leadership. *Family Planning/Population Reporter,* 1976, 5(5), 78–80.

Baer, H. R., & Bush, T. L. *Demographic and economic trends: Social implications for women.* Paper delivered at Canadian Association for American Studies, Tenth Annual Conference, Ottawa, Ontario, October 12, 1974. (Available from Dr. H. R. Kearney, 3358 Woodburn Rd., #31, Annandale, Va. 22003).

Baer, H. R., & Sherif, C. W. (Eds.). A topical bibliography (selectively annotated) on psychology of women. *JSAS Catalog of Selected Documents in Psychology,* 1974, *4,* 42. (MS. No. 614).

Bandura, A., & Walters, R. H. *Social learning and personality development.* New York: Ronald Press, 1963.

Bart, P. B. Sexism and social science: From the guilded cage to the iron cage, or the perils of Pauline. *Journal of Marriage and the Family,* 1971, *33*(4), 734–745. (a)

Bart, P. B. (Ed.). Special issue: Sexism in family studies. *Journal of Marriage and the Family,* 1971, *33*(3), 409–606. (b)

Bell, R. Q. A reinterpretation of the direction of effects in studies of socialization. *Psychological Bulletin,* 1968, *75,* 81–95.

Berlyne, D. *Conflict, arousal, and curiosity.* New York: McGraw-Hill, 1960.

Bernard, J. *The future of motherhood.* New York: Penguin, 1974.

Blake, J. Population policy for Americans: Is the government being misled? *Science,* 1969, *164,* 229.

Bronfenbrenner, U. Toward an experimental ecology of human development. *American Psychologist,* 1977, *32*(7), 513–531.

Callahan, D. *Abortion: Law, choice, and morality.* New York: MacMillan, 1970.

Chesler, P. *Women and madness.* New York: Doubleday, 1972.

Cisler, L. Abortion reform: The new tokenism. *Ramparts,* August 1970, *9*(2), pp. 19–21.

Congress ends abortion fund deadlock. *The Spokeswoman,* January/February 15, 1978, (7–8), pp. 5–6.

Donovan, P. The convention route to an antiabortion amendment: A dangerous tactic. *Family Planning/Population Reporter,* August 1978, *7*(4), 62–64.

Ervin-Tripp, S. M. *Language acquisition and communicative choice.* Stanford: Stanford University Press, 1973.

Etaugh, C. Effects of maternal employment on children: A review of recent research. *Merrill-Palmer Quarterly,* 1974, *20*(2), 71–98.

Etaugh, C., & Spandikow, D. *Attention to sex in psychological research as related to journal policy and author sex.* Paper delivered at National Conference on Feminist Psychology: Research, Theory, and Practice, St. Louis, Missouri, February 6, 1977.

Flexner, E. *Century of struggle.* Cambridge, Mass.: Belknap Press, 1959.

Freeman, J. *The politics of women's liberation.* New York: David McKay, 1975.

Friedan, B. *The feminine mystique.* New York: Dell, 1963.

Gonzales, B., & Ruben, M. (Eds.). Reliance on sterilization expected to increase. *A. V. S. News,* January 1978, p. 3.

Harold, K. Violence against clinics continues. *NARAL Newsletter,* July 1978, *10*(3), pp. 1–2.

Hartup, W. W. Peer relations. In T. D. Spencer & N. Kass (Eds.), *Perspectives in child psychology: Research and review.* New York: McGraw-Hill, 1970, pp. 261–294.

Hebb, D. O. *The organization of behavior.* New York: Wiley, 1949.

Heber, R., Garber, H., Harrington, S., Hoffman, C., & Falender, C. *Rehabilitation of families at risk for mental retardation.* (Progress Report). Madison, Wisconsin: University of Wisconsin, Rehabilitation Research and Training Center in Mental Retardation, December 1972.

Hetherington, E. M. A developmental study of the effects of sex of the dominant parent on sex-role preference, identification, and imitation in children. *Journal of Personality and Social Psychology,* 1965, *2,* 188–194.

Hole, J., & Levine, E. *Rebirth of feminism.* New York: Quadrangle, 1971.

Houseknecht, S. K. Reference group support for voluntary childlessness: Evidence for conformity. *Journal of Marriage and the Family,* 1977, *39*(2), 285–292.

Hunt, J. McV. The psychological basis for using pre-school enrichment as an antidote for cultural deprivation. *Merrill-Palmer Quarterly,* 1964, *10,* 209–248.

Inhelder, B. Memory and intelligence in the child. In D. Elkind & J. H. Flavell (Eds.), *Studies in cognitive development.* New York: Oxford University Press, 1969, pp. 337–364.

Jaffe, F. S., & Dryfoos, J. G. Fertility control services for adolescents: Access and utilization. *Family Planning Perspectives,* 1976, *8*(4), 167–175.

Kanter, R. M. The policy issues: Presentation VI. *Signs: Journal of Women in Culture and Society*, 1976, *1*(3), Part 2, 282-291.

Kohlberg, L. A cognitive-developmental analysis of children's sex role concepts and attitudes. In E. E. Maccoby (Ed.), *The development of sex differences*. Stanford, Calif.: Stanford University Press, 1966, pp. 82-173.

Kreps, J., & Clark, R. *Sex, age, and work*. Baltimore: Johns Hopkins University Press, 1975.

Lamb, M. E. *Development and function of parent-infant relationships in the first two years of life*. Paper delivered at Society for Research in Child Development Conference, New Orleans, Louisiana, March 18, 1977. (a)

Lamb, M. E. *The effects of ecological variables on parent-infant interaction*. Paper delivered at Society for Research in Child Development Conference. New Orleans, Louisiana, March 20, 1977. (b)

Lincoln, R., Döring-Bradley, B., Lindheim, B. L., & Cotterill, M. A. The court, the congress, and the president: Turning back the clock on the pregnant poor. *Family Planning Perspectives*, 1977, *9*(5), 207-214.

Local regulations hinder abortions. *The Nation's Health*, February 1978, pp. 1-2.

Maccoby, E. E., & Feldman, S. S. Mother-attachment and stranger reactions in the third year of life. *Monographs of the society for research in child development*, 1972, *37*(1).

Martin, B. Parent-child relations. In F. D. Horowitz (Ed.), *Review of child development research*. Vol. 4. Chicago: University of Chicago Press, 1975, pp. 463-540.

Moely, B. E. Personal communication. Tulane University, New Orleans, Louisiana, May 2, 1977.

Morgan, R. (Ed.). *Sisterhood is powerful*. New York: Vintage, 1970.

*NOW Bill of Rights*. (B-6/2-74). Chicago: National Organization for Women, 1974.

Mulhauser, K. Personal communication. Letter from Executive Director, National Abortion Rights Action League (NARAL), Washington, D.C., August 2, 1978.

O'Neill, W. L. (Ed.). *The woman movement*. Chicago: Quadrangle, 1969.

Parke, R. D. Personal communication. Society for Research in Child Development Conference, New Orleans, Louisiana, March 17-20, 1977.

Parsons, T., & Bales, R. F. *Family, socialization, and interaction process*. Glencoe, Ill.: Free Press, 1955.

Piaget, J. *The origins of intelligence in the child*. New York: International Universities Press, 1953.

Pleck, J. H., & Sawyer, J. (Eds.). *Men and masculinity*. Englewood Cliffs, New Jersey: Prentice-Hall, 1974.

President's Commission on the Status of Women. *American women*. Washington, D.C. 20210: U.S. Department of Labor, 1963.

Ramirez, F. O., & Weiss, J. A. *A cross-national analysis of the legal status of women*. Paper delivered at the Pacific Sociological Association Meetings, San Diego, California, March 1976. (Available from Dr. Weiss, Department of Sociology, University of Iowa, Iowa City, Iowa 52242).

Ramirez, F. O., Weiss, J. A., & Tracy, T. *The political incorporation of women: A cross-national analysis*. Paper delivered at the American Sociological Association Meetings, San Francisco, California, August 1975. (Available from Dr. Weiss, Department of Sociology, University of Iowa, Iowa City, Iowa 52242).

Rheingold, H. L. To rear a child. *American Psychologist*, January 1973, 42-46.

Ribble, M. A. *Rights of infants*. New York: Columbia University Press, 1943.

Rockefeller, J. D., III, et al. *Population and the American future—The report of the commission on population growth and the American future*. Washington, D.C. 20402: Superintendent of Documents, U. S. Government Printing Office, 1972.

Rosoff, J. I. DHEW issues 'final' abortion regulations. *Planned Parenthood-World Population Washington Memo*, January 27, 1978, p. 1. (b)

Rosoff, J. I. 'Liberalized' antiabortion amendment becomes law after five-month battle. *Planned Parenthood-World Population Washington Memo*, December 16, 1977, pp. 1-2.

Rosoff, J. I. Outlook for 1978 shaped by developments in 1977. *Planned Parenthood-World Population Washington Memo*. January 13, 1978, pp. 3-6. (a)

Rossi, A. Transition to parenthood. *Journal of Marriage and the Family*. February 1968, *30*, 26–39.

Rossi, A. S. Women in the seventies: Problems and possibilities. In *Hearings before the Special Subcommittee on Education of the Committee on Education and Labor*, House of Representatives, 91st Congress, 2nd Session, on Section 805 of H. R. 16098, Part 2, July 1 and 31, 1970, 1062–1077. Washington, D.C.: U. S. Government Printing Office, 1971.

Russo, N. F. The motherhood mandate. *Journal of Social Issues*, 1976, *32*(3), 143–153.

Russo, N. F. On the psychological readiness of students to study population. *Social Education*, April 1972, 357–363.

Sherif, C. W. *Orientation in social psychology*. New York: Harper & Row, 1976.

Sherif, M. & Sherif, C. W. *Reference groups*. New York: Harper & Row, 1964.

Sherman, J. A. *On the psychology of women*. Springfield, Ill.: Charles C. Thomas, 1971.

Shields, S. A. Functionalism, Darwinism, and the psychology of women. A study in social myth. *American Psychologist*, July 1975, 739–754.

Silka, L., & Kiesler, S. Couples who choose to remain childless. *Family Planning Perspectives*, 1977, *9*(1), 16–25.

Sinclair-de-Zwart, H. Developmental linguistics. In E. Elkind & J. H. Flavell (Eds.), *Studies in cognitive development*. New York: Oxford University Press, 1969, pp. 315–336.

Smeal, E. Personal communication. Letter from President, National Organization for Women, Washington, D.C., August 2, 1978.

Spitz, R. A. Hospitalism: An inquiry into the genesis of psychiatric conditions in early childhood. *Psychoanalytic Study of the Child*, 1945, *1*, 53–74.

Stanton, E. C. *Eighty years and more*. New York: Schocken, 1971.

Stein, P. J. *Single*. Englewood Cliffs, New Jersey: Prentice-Hall, 1976.

Stewart, A. J., & Winter, D. G. The nature and causes of female suppression. *Signs: Journal of Women in Culture and Society*, 1977, *2*(3), 531–553.

Tietze, C. Legal abortions in the United States: Rates and ratios by race and age, 1972–1974. *Family Planning Perspectives*, 1977, *9*(1), 12–15. (a)

Tietze, C. New estimates of mortality associated with fertility control. *Family Planning Perspectives*, 1977, *9*(2), 74–76. (b)

Toch, H. *The social psychology of social movements*. New York: Bobbs-Merrill, 1965.

*WEAL's Legislative Program*. Washington, D.C.: Women's Equity Action League, Spring 1977, p. 2.

Weiss, J. A., Ramirez, F. O., & Tracy, T. *Female participation in the occupational system: A comparative institutional analysis*. Paper delivered at Comparative and International Educational Society Meetings, San Francisco, California, March 1975. (Available from Dr. Weiss, Department of Sociology, University of Iowa, Iowa City, Iowa 52242).

Weisstein, N. Kinder, Küche, Kirche as scientific law: Psychology constructs the female. In R. Morgan (Ed.), *Sisterhood is powerful*. New York: Vintage, 1970, pp. 205–220.

White, B. L. *The first three years of life*. Englewood Cliffs, New Jersey: Prentice-Hall, 1975.

Witt, S. H. Native women today: Sexism and the Indian woman. In S. Cox (Ed.), *Female psychology: The emerging self*. Chicago: SRA, 1976.

Yarrow, L. J., Rubenstein, J. L., & Pedersen, F. A. *Infant and environment*. Washington, D.C.: Hemisphere Publishing, 1975.

# Some Social Implications of Sex-Choice Technology

Linda Fidell, Donnie Hoffman, and Patti Keith-Spiegel

*California State University, Northridge*

A survey of 710 undergraduates was conducted to assess the probable patterns of utilization of sex-choice technology when it becomes widely available. Ideal family composition was determined along with demographic and attitudinal variables. Results confirmed the overwhelming preference for male children, in general, and male firstborn children, in particular: 85% wanted a firstborn boy, while 73% wanted a secondborn girl. Reasons for the choice reflected both considerable knowledge of advantages accruing to first-born children and stereotypic expectations regarding sons and daughters. The possible consequences of widespread use of sex choice technology for women's civil rights are discussed.

Technological advances have frequently had social implications that were poorly understood prior to their implementation. This paper examines the possible social consequences of utilization of sex-choice technology before it becomes widely available. The specific focus of analysis is the effect of the widespread use of sex-choice techniques on the status of women and egalitarian sex roles.

Methods for controlling the sex of offspring are being actively researched. Procedures for separating male from female sperm range from differential sedimentation through centrifugation, controlling the pH of vaginal secretions, critical timing of intercourse, and a host of other likely possibilities. Shettles (see Rorvik, 1970) claims that a combination of several of these procedures can be practiced relatively easily by lay persons at home and is currently 80 to 85% effective. A half-page advertisement in a Sunday magazine newspaper supplement was recently brought to the authors' attention. The

---

Donnie Hoffman is now at the University of California at Santa Barbara. Reprint requests should be directed to Linda Fidell, California State University, Northridge CA. 91330.

*Psychology of Women Quarterly, Vol. 4(1) Fall 1979*
0361-6843/79/1500-0032$00.95 © 1979 Human Sciences Press

LINDA FIDELL, DONNIE HOFFMAN, AND PATTI KEITH-SPIEGEL

advertisement, entitled "Choosex," offers assistance (for a fee) for predetermining the sex of offspring. Despite some argument over claims for this procedure it seems likely that at least one effective method will be available within the next few years and that, if the method is convenient and inexpensive, it will be widely used (Etzioni, 1968).

Public attention has been drawn to two recently developed procedures which might be used to determine the sex of children. Undocumented assertions have been made that amniocentesis, in conjunction with abortion if results indicated the fetus was not of the desired sex, has already been used to ensure the sex of the child. Fetal implantation has a similar potential application.

Previous research has pointed to the overwhelming preference for male children in general (Dinitz, Dynes, & Clarke, 1954; Hammer, 1970; Markle & Nam, 1971; Gordon, Gordon, & Gunther, 1964; Gillman, 1968), and male firstborn children in particular (Buckhout, 1972). Several researchers (Altus, 1966; Boroson, 1974; Etzioni, 1968; Largey, 1973; Westoff & Rindfuss, 1974) have pointed to a variety of social implications that may result from widespread use of sex-choice techniques and a higher overall production of males, e.g., heightened aggressiveness among males in competition for scarcer females. But, to our knowledge, no one as yet has considered the consequences of confounding birth order with sex of offspring, a confounding which will occur if people use sex-choice technology to ensure that a male child is born first. Nor has the relationship between sex-choice and family patterning been related to attitudes towards the women's civil rights movement.

Birth order has been reliably associated with other variables in numerous studies. Causal links between birth order and various aspects of behavior have been attributed to biology (Boroson, 1974; Stone & Rowley, 1966), maternal behavior (Palmer, 1966; Sears, Maccoby, & Levin, 1957), behavior of the older sibling (Jacobs & Moss, 1974), number of other siblings (Zajonc & Markus, 1975), and confounding between family size and socioeconomic status (Schooler, 1972). However, although the exact mechanisms by which birth order exerts its effect remain unclear, research has demonstrated that firstborn children tend to behave differently from laterborn children in a variety of ways.

Both firstborn and secondborn children appear to have certain advantages and disadvantages. On the positive side, firstborn children of either sex have been found to be more achievement oriented, ambitious, conscientious, self-confident (Boroson, 1974), creative

(Lichtenwalner & Maxwell, 1969), verbal (Rosenberg & Sutton-Smith, 1966), intelligent (Belmont & Marolla, 1973), self-controlled, serious, and adult oriented (Arrowood & Amaroso, 1965; Becker, Lerner, & Carroll, 1966; Carringan & Julian, 1966) than laterborns. In addition, they are more likely to attend college and are overrepresented in positions of academic and professional achievement and eminence (Boroson, 1974; Warren, 1966). Somewhat less favorably, firstborns have also been described as more conforming (Becker, Lerner, & Carroll, 1966) and susceptible to social pressures (Arrowood & Amaroso, 1965; Carringan & Julian, 1966; Warren, 1966), more affiliative and dependent (Schachter, 1959; Sears, 1950; see also Conners, 1963, for a reversal of this finding), and more anxious (Schachter, 1959).

Secondborn children of either sex have been described as more cheerful and easygoing, popular, practical and action oriented (Boroson, 1974), likely to seek help and adult approval, and more talkative than firstborns (McGurk & Lewis, 1972). They also tend to display more nervous habits (Koch, 1956) and greater need for affiliation, if not greater expectation of affiliative rewards (Conners, 1963).

Notice that there is a tendency for firstborn children of either sex to resemble the masculine sex role stereotype and for secondborn children of either sex to resemble the feminine sex role stereotype. This effect may be amplified when the firstborn child actually is a male with the secondborn child female (Doren, 1973; Lunneborg, 1968). However, the effect may be weakened by the tendency of opposite sex siblings to have less well-defined sex-typing than same sex siblings (Heilbrun & Fromme, 1965; Kammey, 1966; Sutton-Smith & Rosenberg, 1965).[1] Similarly, the effect, at least with respect to intellectual development, may be weakened by increasing the spacing between children (Zajonc & Marcus, 1975).

Firstborn men, in particular, have been described as showing intellectual interests (Oberlander, Frauenfelder, & Heath, 1971), unlikely to seek affection, untalkative and unconforming to instructions, and unlikely to display negative affect (McGurk & Lewis, 1972).

Secondborn women, in particular, have been described by Brim (1958) as both more masculine (an effect due to an older brother) and more feminine (an effect of being the younger child). On the other hand, Douvan and Adelson (1966) concluded that the younger sisters of older brothers were the most traditionally feminine of all the chil-

---

[1]Opposite sex siblings also showed more neuroticism than same sex siblings on the Eysenck Personality Inventory while firstborn males and secondborn females showed more extraversion than firstborn females and secondborn males (McCormick & Baer, 1975).

LINDA FIDELL, DONNIE HOFFMAN, AND PATTI KEITH-SPIEGEL

dren they studied. Secondborn women have also been described as showing social, as opposed to intellectual, interests (Oberlander, et al., 1971) and as likely to engage in feminine role playing, to withdraw from aggressive encounters, to seek approval, and to display positive affect (McGurk & Lewis, 1972).

Thus, one effect of confounding birth order with sex of offspring by use of sex-choice technology may be to amplify or to create real differences in sex-typing.

One purpose of the present study is to determine if educated young people, who will soon start families and who have presumably been exposed to feminist issues, including sex-role stereotyping, continue to prefer male (firstborn) children. We also set out to investigate the relationship between the sex preferences and certain demographic and attitudinal variables, to determine the strength of the preferences, and to ascertain the reasons for the preferences.

## METHOD

A paper and pencil survey was conducted among 710 undergraduate students (409 women and 301 men) during 1973 and 1974. Analysis of the responses to standard demographic questions revealed that most of the respondents were in the first three years of college, moderate to liberal in political persuasion, 85% white, 93% single, and roughly evenly spread among Protestants (27%), Catholics (18%), Jews (25%), and "none" or "other" (29%). All were residents of the San Fernando Valley, a suburban area near Los Angeles which has predominantly working and middle class residents.

Attitudes toward the women's civil rights movement were also assessed. Finally, information concerning preferred family patterns (number of children desired, sex preference for children in each birth order, and desired parental age at birth of each child) was collected.

A subsample of 227 of the respondents received a more lengthy questionnaire containing the items listed above together with items designed to reveal the strength of the family pattern preferences, the likelihood of employing sex-choice techniques to ensure the preference, and the reasons or perceived advantages and disadvantages of the preference.

## RESULTS

If all of the desired children were born to these respondents, there would be 1,681 births. Of these specified births, 919 (55%) were boys and 762 (45%) were girls. The respondents would have, on average, 2.4 children, with 57.2% of the respondents wishing to produce exactly two children. Because this was the modal response, and because of the trend toward two-child families, the remainder of our analyses focus on this family pattern.

The respondents also anticipated being, on average, 25.5 years of age at the birth of the first child and 27.9 years of age at the birth of the second, with the mother projected as two years younger than the father at the time of both births. These projections appear to be similar, though somewhat later, to actual census data for this cohort (U.S. Bureau of the Census, 1975).

A strong relationship showing the desire for firstborn males and secondborn females was found (see Table 1). The value of the chi square test of association between desired sex of child and birth order of child was 440.54, 1 $df$, $p<0.001$.

The male and female respondents in this study did not significantly differ in demographic characteristics, number of children desired, or desired sex of firstborn child. That is, women did not tend to desire a firstborn son any more or less frequently than did men. The women were, however, more inclined to favorable attitudes toward women's civil rights than were the men, $X^2 = 11.97$, 5 $df$, $p<.05$. More women were inclined to check that they "strongly approve" of the women's civil rights movement while more men were likely to "slightly" or "generally disapprove."

There were no significant differences in desired sex of the firstborn child in this rather homogeneous college-age sample. The desired sex of firstborn child was unrelated to educational level, political persuasion, racial heritage, religious preference, and marital status.

There were differences, however, among those with varying attitudes toward the women's civil rights movement. First, those who

TABLE ONE

RELATIONSHIP BETWEEN DESIRED SEX OF CHILD

AND BIRTH ORDER OF CHILD

|  |  | Birth Order | |  |
|---|---|---|---|---|
|  |  | Firstborn | Secondborn |  |
| Desired Sex | Male | 561  (372.8)* | 174  (362.2) | 735 |
|  | Female | 102  (290.2) | 470  (281.8) | 572 |
|  |  | 663 | 644 | 1307 |

Chi Square = 440.54, 1 df, p<0.001

*Expected Frequencies

"strongly approved" of the goals of the movement were much more likely to state that they did not desire children at all. The chi square value between number of children desired and attitudes toward the movement (collapsing the "strongly disapprove" with "disapprove" responses to meet expected frequency requirements) was 46.08, 3 $df$, $p<0.001$.

Secondly, there was an association between the desired sex of firstborn and attitudes toward women's civil rights (see Table 2). Those respondents who "strongly approved" and, interestingly, those who "strongly disapproved" of the goals of the women's civil rights movement were both more likely to desire a girl as a firstborn child (although, overall, they still preferred a boy). The respondents with intermediate attitudes toward women's civil rights were consistent in the ratio of their preference for a male firstborn child.

The strength of the preference for specified family pattern (measured in the subsample) was ascertained by asking whether or not respondents would consider using sex-chioce methods and how much effort they would expend to use the techniques. Sixty percent of the respondents indicated that they would probably not use sex-choice methods while 29% said they probably would, and 11% said they would use them to guarantee that the second child was of opposite sex to the first. As to effort, 35% reported that they would exert "none," 14% said "a little," 22% reported "some," 22% "a moderate amount," and 8% "a great deal." Most respondents also reported that they would compromise their preference with a mate who felt differently.

Lastly, the subsample of respondents was asked to give the rea-

TABLE TWO

RELATIONSHIP BETWEEN ATTITUDES TOWARD WOMEN'S CIVIL RIGHTS AND
DESIRED SEX OF FIRSTBORN CHILD

| | | Strongly Disapprove | Generally Disapprove | Slightly Disapprove | Slightly Approve | Generally Approve | Strongly Approve | Total |
|---|---|---|---|---|---|---|---|---|
| | Male | 13 (16.1)* | 67 (65.3) | 50 (47.5) | 150 (143.3) | 228 (222.9) | 32 (44.9) | 540 |
| Desired Sex of Firstborn | | | | | | | | |
| | Female | 6 (2.9) | 10 (11.7) | 6 (8.5) | 19 (25.7) | 35 (40.0) | 21 (8.1) | 97 |
| | TOTAL | ·19 | 77 | 56 | 169 | 263 | 53 | 637 ** |

Chi Square = 32.22, 5 df, p⟨0.001

* Expected Frequencies

** Several respondents stated no opinion

PSYCHOLOGY OF WOMEN QUARTERLY

TABLE THREE

REASONS/ADVANTAGES FOR SELECTION OF SEX OF FIRSTBORN

| Reasons or Advantages | Sex Preference Male | Female |
|---|---|---|
| For the firstborn child - | | |
| to provide him or her with practical or psychological advantages of firstborn status | 26% | 20% |
| For the younger sibling | 11% | 20% |
| to provide protection for younger sibling | 2% | 0% |
| to provide instruction for younger sibling | 3% | 7% |
| to help care for younger sibling | 2% | 13% |
| to provide social introductions for younger sibling | 4% | 0% |
| For the parents | 39% | 27% |
| to carry on the family name | 4% | 0% |
| to replicate family pattern of respondent's family | 3% | 3% |
| for parental ego needs or pleasures | 23% | 7% |
| to provide an "easy" child to rear | 9% | 17% |
| For "no special reason" | 25% | 33% |

sons or the advantages they saw to the sex of the firstborn child which they had specified. The reasons (offered by all but 6 of the 227 respondents) are collapsed into large categories by desired sex of firstborn and presented in Table 3.

## DISCUSSION

Should effective sex-choice techniques be practiced by these respondents to produce their family patterns desired at this time, 55% of the children born would be boys; 85% of the firstborn children would be boys, with 73% of the secondborn children girls. These findings replicate those of earlier studies, showing an overall preference for male children, and an overwhelming preference for male firstborn children. Confounding between birth order and sex of offspring would occur with the likely consequence of strengthening or creating sex differences where they currently are not reliably found (Maccoby & Jacklin, 1974). Because the behavior of first and secondborn children is consistent with stereotypes about men and women, it seems likely that the behavioral differences would be attributed to biological differences between the sexes rather than to birth order effects.

With respect to parental age, it is important to note that not only will the girl be born second, but also she will be born, on the average, to older parents. Stone and Rowley (1966) concluded that increasing maternal age at birth of child was associated with decreasing intelligence and and longevity, and increasing congenital malformations, mongolism, mental disorders, neuroticism, and personality and conduct disorders among offspring. Although girls probably are biologically stronger than are boys (Barfield, 1976), it would be unfortunate to systematically pair the sex of the child with the disadvantages associated with increasing parental age. We recognize, however, that most of the respondents in our sample, *if* their preferred pattern is followed, will have completed their families prior to the middle-thirties when deleterious effects of maternal age increase sharply.

Improved status of women and egalitarian sex roles might be fostered by use of sex-choice techniques if people would not need to "keep trying again" to get the opposite sex child. Fewer children would be born (Westoff, Potter, & Sagi, 1963), resulting in increased free time for women to pursue their own goals. Family satisfaction might also increase, with benefit to both parents and offspring.

There was no difference in preference for boys and for male firstborn children among those who otherwise differed in demographic characteristics (within the limits found in a routine college population). This finding is consistent with that of Markle and Nam (1971), who found a strong preference for boys even among their non-college sample, but not with that of Hammer (1970), who found that non-college women preferred to have a girl. This pattern of results suggests, at least, that the college-educated, middle class respondent, the kind of respondent who is most likely to use sex-choice techniques, has a strong preference for a male firstborn child.

Women shared with men the preference for male (firstborn) offspring. The only group among whom the preference appeared weakened was among those who "strongly approved" of the goals of the women's civil rights movement. However, almost a third of the people who "strongly approved" of the goals of the movement, also stated that they did not want children (compared to 8% overall who did not want children). Thus, many of the strongest supporters of feminism may not be in the "family business" at all. Their influence may, then, be relatively isolated from the transmission of "non-status-quo" sex-choice and family patterning attitudes from generation to generation.

With respect to the reasons for desiring firstborn boys or girls, it is fairly clear that about 25% of the respondents understood that being a firstborn conveys some advantages and wanted, for the most part, to give these advantages to boys. They also desired firstborn sons to meet parental ego needs and for parental pleasure. It is interesting to note that respondents were more frequently able to supply a reason for wanting a firstborn son than for wanting a firstborn daughter. Among those who wanted firstborn daughters, leading reasons were to help care for younger siblings and to provide the parents with an easy child to rear.

It would appear, from the answers to questions about strength of preference, that respondents do not feel strongly about their ideal family plan, would likely not go to special efforts to bring the plan about, and would readily compromise with a mate of differing views. Largey (1972) reports data which suggest that only a small percentage of the population would be able to agree with their mates on the sex of the child and then, that it would be acceptable to use one or more sex-choice methods to ensure the child's sex. However, this situation may change as the technology becomes available, particularly if it is easy and inexpensive to use, despite the fact that 60% of our sample claimed they would not make use of sex-choice methods. Etzioni (1968) predicts widespread use of the techniques, since it seems likely that when people become aware that they have a choice, they will feel more strongly about making it. One interesting aside is that whatever methods become available, they will likely require some forethought. If a large percentage of births remain unplanned, then the social effects of sex-choice technology would be considerably limited.

On balance, we judge that the use of sex-choice techniques is likely to be much more harmful than helpful to the goals of increasing the status of women and egalitarian sex roles. Use of the techniques may produce more "masculine men" and "feminine women" than are found currently (Bem, 1975), with corresponding increases in behavioral rigidity among those who are strongly sex-typed.

How can the stereotyping effects of confounding sex with birth order be minimized? One alternative is to ban the use of the technique. However, we prefer to suggest promotion of an attitude favorable to the selection of the sex of the second child, but not the first. This would avoid confounding sex with birth order while allowing people to guarantee variety in the sex of their children. Encouraging feminists to have children might even be considered, because it may strengthen the preference for firstborn daughters. In addition, Zajonc and Markus (1975) present evidence to suggest that birth order effects can be minimized by spacing children four or more years apart. Thus, even if sex-choice techniques are used to ensure firstborn son and secondborn daughter, the effects of confounding sex and birth order can be buffered by having the second child at least four years after the first child. Of course, the best solution for women, the children, and society in general is to eliminate sex role stereotyping so that sons are not desired over daughters.

We believe that the implications of the technology need to be clearly understood, and the techniques judiciously applied, so as not to undermine the success women have begun to achieve.

## REFERENCES

Altus, W. Birth order and its sequelae. *Science,* 1966, *151* (3706), 44-49.

Arrowood, A., & Amaroso, D. Social comparison and ordinal position. *Journal of Personality and Social Psychology,* 1965, *2,* 101-104.

Barfield, A. Biological influences on sex differences in behavior. In M. S. Teitelbaum (Ed.), *Sex Differences.* Garden City, N.Y.: Anchor Press, 1976.

Becker, S. W., Lerner, M. J., & Carroll, J. Conformity as a function of birth order and type of group pressure: A verification. *Journal of Personality and Social Psychology,* 1966, *3,* 242-249.

Belmont, L., & Marolla, F. A. Birth order, family size, and intelligence. *Science,* 1973, *182,* 1096.

Bem, S. L. Sex role adaptability: One consequence of psychological androgyny. *Journal of Personality and Social Psychology,* 1975, *31*(4), 634-643.

Boroson, W. First-Born—Fortune's favorite? *Readings in Human Development '74/'75.* 1974, Guilford, Connecticut, 134-138.

Brim, O. G., Jr. Family structure and sex pure learning by children: A further analysis of Helen Koch's Data. *Sociometry,* 1958, *21*(1), 1-17.

Buckhout, R. Toward a two-child norm: Changing family planning attitudes. *American Psychologist,* 1972, *27*(1), 16-26.

Carringan, W., & Julian, J. Sex and birth order differences in conformity: Function of need affiliation arousal. *Journal of Personality and Social Psychology,* 1966, *3,* 479-483.

Conners, C. K. Birth order and needs for affiliation. *Journal of Personality,* 1963, *31,* 408-416.

Dinitz, S., Dynes, R., & Clarke, A. Preferences for male or female children: Traditional or affectional? *Marriage and Family Living,* 1954, *16,* 128-130.

Doren, M. Evaluation of studies on birth order and sibling position. *Dissertation Abstracts International,* 1973, *33* (10-A), 5543-5549.

Douvan, E., & Adelson, J. *The Adolescent Experience.* New York: Wiley, 1966.

Etzioni, A. Sex control, science, and society. *Science,* 1968, *161,* 1107-1112.

Gillman, R. D. The dreams of pregnant women and maternal adaptation. *American Journal of Orthopsychiatry,* 1968, *38,* 688-692.

Gordon, K., Gordon, R., & Gunther, M. *The split-level trap.* New York: Dell, 1964.

Hammer, M. Preference for a male child: Cultural factor. *Journal of Individual Psychology,* 1970, *26,* 54-56.

Heibrun, A. B., Jr., & Fromme, D. K. Parental identification of late adolescents and level of adjustment: The importance of parent-model attributes, ordinal position, and sex of the child. *The Journal of Genetic Psychology,* 1965, *107,* 49-59.

Jacobs, B., & Moss, H. Birth order and sex of siblings as determinants of mother-infant interaction. Paper delivered at the American Psychological Association meetings, New Orleans, 1974.

Kammey, R. K. Birth order and the feminine sex role among college women. *American Sociological Review,* 1966, *31*(2), 508-515.

Koch, H. L. Some emotional attitudes of the young child in relation to characteristics of his sibling. *Child Development,* 1956, *27,* 393-426.

Largey, G. Sociological aspects of sex pre-selection: A study of the acceptance of a medical innovation. Doctoral dissertation, Department of Sociology, State University of New York at Buffalo, 1972.

Largey, G. Sex control and society: A critical assessment of sociological speculations. *Social Problems,* 1973, *20*(3), 310-318.

Lichtenwalner, J., & Maxwell, J. The relationship of birth order and socio-economic status to the creativity of preschool children. *Child Development,* 1969, *40,* 1241-1247.

Lunneborg, P. Birth order, aptitude, and achievement. *Journal of Consulting and Clinical Psychology,* 1968, *32*(1), 101.

Maccoby, E. E., & Jacklin, C. N. *The Psychology of Sex Differences.* Stanford, Calif.: Stanford University Press, 1974.

Markle, G. E., & Nam, C. B. Sex predetermination: Its impact on fertility. *Social Biology,* 1971, *18,* 73.

McCormick, K. & Baer, D. J. Birth order, sex of subject, and sex of sibling as factors in extraversion and neuroticism in two-child families. *Psychological Reports,* 1975, *37,* 259-261.

McGurk, H., & Lewis, M. Birth order: A phenomenon in search of an explanation. ERIC, ED 067156, 1972.

Oberlander, M., Frauenfelder, K., & Heath, H. The relationship of ordinal position and sex to interest patterns. *The Journal of Genetic Psychology,* 1971, *119,* 29-36.

Palmer, R. D. Birth order and identification. *Journal of Consulting Psychology,* 1966, *30*(2), 129-135.

Rorvik, D. *Your baby's sex: Now you can choose.* New York: Dodd, Mead and Co., 1970.

Rosenberg, B. G., & Sutton-Smith, B. Sibling association, family size, and cognitive abilities. *Journal of Genetic Psychology,* 1966, *109,* 271-279.

Schachter, S. *The Psychology of Affiliation.* Stanford, Calif.: Stanford University Press, 1959.

Schooler, C. Birth order effects: Not here, not now! *Psychological Bulletin,* 1972, *78*(3), 161-175.

Sears, R. R. Ordinal position in the family as a psychological variable. *American Sociological Review,* 1950, *15,* 397-401.

Sears, R. R., Maccoby, E., & Levin, H. *Patterns of Child Rearing.* Evanston, Ill.: Row, Peterson, 1957.

Stone, F. B., & Rowley, V. N. Children's behavior problems and mother's age. *The Journal of Psychology,* 1966, *63,* 229-233.

Sutton-Smith, B., & Rosenberg, B. G. Age changes in the effects of ordinal position in sex-role identification. *The Journal of Genetic Psychology,* 1965, *107,* 61-73.

U.S. Bureau of the Census, *Current Population Reports.* Series P-20, No. 315, Trends in childspacing, June 1975.

Warren, R. Birth order and social behavior. *Psychological Bulletin,* 1966, *65*(1), 38-49.

Westoff, C. F., Potter, R. G., Jr., & Sagi, P. C. *The third child.* Princeton, N.J.: Princeton University Press, 1963.

Westoff, C. F., & Rindfuss, R. Sex preselection in the United States: Some implications. *Science,* 1974, *184*(4137), 633-636.

Zajonc, R. B., & Markus, G. B. Birth order and intellectual development. *Psychological Review,* 1975, *82*(1), 74-88.

# The Relationship Between Sex Roles, Fertility, and Family Size Preferences

Linda J. Beckman

*University of California, Los Angeles*

Interviews regarding sex-role attitudes, sex-role behaviors, fertility, and fertility preferences were conducted with 583 currently married women aged 18 through 49. Separate correlational analyses for blacks, Anglos, and Hispanic women revealed that for Anglos and blacks sex-role attitudes appeared to be more highly associated with children raised and desired fertility than did division of household tasks and decisions. Past and present role behavior outside of the family (i.e., employment experience) were related to fertility and fertility preferences for all three groups. A path analysis, applied for Anglos only, indicated that number of children raised may influence sex-role behavior and attitudes which, in turn, may influence current fertility desires. However, the variable with the largest direct effect on total children desired was the number of children one already has. Various dimensions of sex roles influenced fertility desires in different ways. Traditionalism of attitudes had a positive effect while relative performance of feminine tasks had a negative effect on total number of children wanted.

Sex roles have in the past been conceptualized in a variety of ways. Although most studies have included only one dimension, sex roles are best considered as multidimensional, including both perceptions of women's roles and women's actual role behavior. Researchers generally have found a moderate relationship between sex-role attitudes and fertility. Women who are less sex-role tra-

---

This research was supported by Grant HD-07323 and Contract HD-52807 from the Center for Population Research of the National Institute of Child Health and Human Development, and by a Research Career Development Award (K02-AA00002) to the author. Tom Day, Leigh Burstein, and Betsy Bosak Houser provided helpful comments regarding the manuscript. Computer assistance was provided by the UCLA Health Sciences Computing Facility, supported by NIH Special Research Resource Grant RR-3.

ditional in attitudes have lower actual fertility (i.e., number of children born or raised [Haas, 1972; Scanzoni, 1975]). A negative relationship between liberal sex-role definitions and fertility orientations (i.e., intentions, desires, and preferences regarding family size) has been found for both university students (Fox, 1977) and married couples (Scanzoni, 1976).

It is generally hypothesized that women who adopt modern roles or see modern roles such as full-time employment as desirable will tend to produce fewer children because of the incompatibility of the traditional role of mother with the more modern roles (Beckman, 1978; Turner & Simmons, in press). Research shows that even women who desire jobs considered nontraditional for women do not reject the core female roles of wife and mother. However, they do expect to have fewer children than do more traditional women (Tangri, 1972). Many studies show negative relationships between women's labor force participation and fertility variables such as family size intentions (e.g., Siegel & Haas, 1963; Ryder & Westoff, 1971). Scanzoni (1976) has shown that in households where the wife works full-time, gender status, i.e., the wife as junior partner or equal partner, has a more significant impact on birth orientations.

As previously stated, sex-role variables have several distinct dimensions. All dimensions of sex roles, however, characterize individuals on a continuum according to degree of sex-role traditionalism (or its opposite, sex-role modernity). Traditionalism is associated with the preeminence of the wife-mother role and rejection of role behaviors for women such as independence, equal status, and authority with men. Reported perceptions regarding role behavior for women can be distinguished from reported actual role behaviors among women. In the present study, reported perceptions are conceptualized into two dimensions: attitudes regarding women's roles (e.g., does a woman agree that "it is better for all concerned if the wife stays home and cares for the children while the husband works"?), and perceptions regarding own sex-role orientation toward career (e.g., does a woman consider herself to be highly career oriented?), and homemaking. Additional dimensions of sex-role perceptions, however, have also been suggested. For instance, Turner and Simmons (in press) consider sex-role self-concept (e.g., does a woman consider herself to possess traditional feminine attributes?), and the value of children (i.e., how positively the rewards of children are perceived) as measures of sex-role values.

Sex-role behaviors can be divided into behaviors within and behaviors outside of the family. (Although the attitudinal dimension also could have been divided into intra- and extra-family categories, this distinction is not considered in the present paper, because the scale used deals with the interaction of roles.) While studies on fertility usually have considered whether or not the wife adopts the role option of employment outside the family (e.g., Scanzoni, 1976; Terry, 1975), role behavior within the family generally has been ignored.

In the present study, measures of both sex-role perceptions and sex-role behaviors are considered. Measures of perceptions include sex-role attitudes and sex-role orientation, while measures of behavior include both utilization of role options outside the family and sex-role relationships (such as division of tasks and decision making) within the marital dyad. It is not assumed that all of these sex-role measures have a similar relationship to fertility or fertility preferences. Recent analyses of sex roles suggest that these dimensions often may not be intercorrelated (Havro-Mannila, 1969; Beckman & Houser, in press), and it is not expected that they all affect fertility variables in the same way.

Furthermore, causality is most likely reciprocal—sex-role dimensions influence fertility variables and fertility variables influence sex roles. The assumption of most previous studies has been that sex roles influence fertility or fertility preferences. Although one study which took the opposite approach found little evidence that fertility influenced sex roles (Turner & Simmons, in press), it still is probable that the number of children women have can affect the roles available to them both within and outside of the family.

The proposed model is as follows: At any given point in time, a woman's fertility (up to that point) may influence one or more of the sex-role dimensions. Because fertility is one of a large number of variables affecting sex roles, it may account for only a limited amount of the variance in sex roles. It is tentatively hypothesized that sex-role *behaviors* affect fertility preferences rather than vice versa. Similarly, although sex-role attitudes and fertility preferences are likely to mutually affect each other, for purposes of our analyses it is assumed that sex-role attitudes more directly affect fertility preferences rather than vice versa.

Background factors such as age, education, or socioeconomic status have been shown to influence sex roles (e.g., Beckman & Houser, in press); this influence may be either direct or indirect. If these demographic variables affect both fertility and sex roles, the apparent relationship between fertility (or fertility preferences) and sex roles may be spurious. Similarly, the apparent relationship between sex-role variables and fertility preferences would be spurious, if sex-role variables have no effect on fertility preferences when past fertility is controlled. If sex-role variables do not add to the proportion of the variance explained in fertility preferences after background factors and prior fertility behavior have been controlled, it suggests that sex-role dimensions do not have an independent effect on fertility preferences.

The present study examines the relationship between fertility variables and various dimensions of sex roles among a Los Angeles County representative sample of married women in their childbearing years. In addition to a correlational analysis, the causal networks connecting sex-role, fertility, and background variables will be examined. For purposes of this causal analysis it is hypothesized as follows:

1) Sociodemographic variables (e.g., age, education, socioeconomic status) influence both fertility and sex roles.

2) Past fertility (i.e., number of children raised) directly (a) negatively influences sex-role behaviors outside the family (e.g., employment status); (b) positively affects sex-role attitudes; but (c) only indirectly influences sex-role behaviors within the family.

3) Traditionalism in sex-role attitudes: (a) negatively influences employment status and egalitarian sex-role behaviors within the family (e.g., husband's performance of traditionally feminine tasks); and (b) is positively related to fertility preferences (i.e., number of children wanted and additional children wanted).

4) Employment status, a measure of sex-role behavior outside the family, positively influences egalitarian sex-role behaviors in the family.

5) Non-traditional or egalitarian sex-role behaviors, both within and outside of the family, negatively affect fertility preferences.

## METHOD

### Procedures

A Los Angeles County representative area probability sample of 583 women aged 18 through 49, currently married and living with spouse, was selected, using the Los Angeles Metropolitan Area Survey (LAMAS) sampling frame. The respondents' average age was 34.0; their average number of years of education was 12.44; and their average family income before taxes in 1973 was $17,469. Ninety-four percent of the women had at some time been employed; and 46.4 percent were currently employed. Sixty-one percent were Anglo; 23 percent had Spanish surnames; and 9 percent were black.

A letter was sent to all households selected through the sampling procedures to provide an overview of the study and inform the residents that an interviewer would be contacting them. Interviewers were required to make five callbacks at various times at each residence, if necessary, to obtain screening data for determination of eligibility and to contact an eligible respondent. Female interviewers followed a standardized schedule of structured and open-ended questions; interviews took an average of 70 minutes to complete.

## Instruments

The questions of relevance to the present paper include those measuring:

1) Reported sex-role perceptions including (a) attitudes and (b) own sex-role orientations;
2) Sex-role behaviors, including (a) role behaviors in the marital dyad and (b) role behaviors outside the dyad;
3) Fertility behavior and preferences;
4) Sociodemographic variables.

*Sex-Role Attitudes (Sex-Role Perceptions).* A sex-role attitude scale consisted of eight items rated on four-point scales from (1) strongly agree to (4) strongly disagree. Typical items were: (1) a pre-school child is likely to suffer if his/her mother works; (2) it is much better for everyone involved if the man is the achiever outside the home and the woman takes care of the home and family; and (3) if a husband and wife both have full-time jobs, the husband should devote just as much time to household tasks as the wife. The items were selected from the Mason and Bumpass (1975) Sex-Role Scale (six items) and from Spence and Helmreich's (1972) Attitudes Toward Women Scale (two items). This particular set of items was chosen because it was preferable to select items that dealt specifically with the interaction of employment and family roles and also with sex-role division of labor. Scores on individual items were transformed where necessary so that high scores indicated a highly traditional response and the scores on the eight items could be combined into an overall attitudinal "traditionalism" index.

*Own Sex-Role Orientation (Sex-Role Perceptions).* Career orientation was assessed by having respondents rate themselves on a five-point scale from (1) not at all career-oriented, through (3) somewhat career-oriented, to (5) extremely career-oriented. Homemaker orientation was assessed in a similar manner.

*Sex-Role Behavior in the Marital Dyad.* Sex-role behavior within the marital dyad was assessed by the indices which measured reported division of masculine tasks, reported division of feminine tasks, and reported division of decision making in the dyad. Task performance and decision making were rated on a five-point scale of (1) husband always, (2) husband more than wife, (3) each equally, (4) wife more than husband, and (5) wife always. Task items included six traditionally feminine tasks (cooking, washing dishes, washing clothes, cleaning house, marketing, and taking care of the children, if the respondent had children), and four traditionally masculine tasks (getting the car fixed, repairing things around the house, moving heavy pieces of furniture, and mowing the lawn). The eight decision items were: disciplining the children (if the respondent had children); how many children to have; where to go on vacation; what house or apartment to live in; how to spend the family income; which job the husband takes; whether or not the wife works; and which friends to see. Five of the items (house or apartment, vacation, husband's job, mowing lawn, dishes) are the same as those used in the original Blood and Wolfe (1960) study of family behavior. The additional items were added in order to provide a more representative group of tasks and decisions.

Items were combined into three summary indices (each of which consisted of the mean value of all index items for which data were available): Masculine Tasks, Feminine Tasks, and Decisions. The higher the score on each of these indices the greater the relative participation of the wife.

*Sex-Role Behavior Outside the Marital Dyad.* Non-family role options were assessed through two measures of employment experience: Employment status and percentage of time employed during marriage. Respondents indicated their employment history and from their responses their employment status was categorized as either currently employed full-time, currently employed part-time, currently unemployed, and never employed. Past employment experience was also assessed through the percentage of time the respondent had worked during present and past marriages. The percentage of time worked was weighted accordingly for full-time and part-time (considered as 50% time) employment.

*Fertility Behavior and Preferences.* Four fertility variables were measured: past fertility, total number of children wanted, additional children wanted, and preference for sex composition. The index of past fertility used was number of children raised. All children who were either born to, adopted, or raised (e.g., step-children) by the respondent were included in this index of fertility. Fertility preferences were assessed through questions concerning number of children wanted and additional children wanted. Total number of children wanted was measured by the question "If you could have just what you wanted, altogether how many children, both your own and adopted, would you like to have?" Number of additional children wanted was equal to "total number of children wanted" minus "number of children raised." The number of boys minus the number of girls (from the question "If you could have just what you wanted, how many boys and how many girls would you like?") was used as a measure of preference for sex composition that controlled to some extent for total family size desired.

*Sociodemographic Variables.* The three sociodemographic variables measured in the present study are age, education and husband's socioeconomic status. The socioeconomic status indicator used—the Duncan Socioeconomic Index—is computed from occupational prestige ratings and average income and educational levels for occupational categories.

# RESULTS

## Correlational Analysis

Zero-order correlations between variables of interest are presented in Tables 1–3. Because of the large number of variables, only three key sociodemographic variables are included. Because women in different ethnic groups may differ in fertility, sex-role attitudes and behaviors (Houser & Beckman, in press), labor force participation rates, educational history, and socioeconomic status, separate analyses were computed for Anglos, blacks, and Latinos. In general, correlations between sex role and fertility variables were highest for blacks and lowest for Latinos.

Correlations for Anglos are presented in Table 1. The moderate correlations between the various dimensions of sex roles (middle portion of Table 1) indicate that these dimensions, although related to one general concept, are distinct. As these relationships have been previously considered (Beckman & Houser, in press), they are not further discussed in this section of the present paper.

The dimensions of sex roles most closely related to actual number of children raised for Anglos were role options outside of the

Table 1. Correlations Between Sex-Role & Fertility Variables for Anglos (N = 359)[a]

|  | (1) | (2) | (3) | (4) | (5) | (6) | (7) | (8) | (9) | (10) | (11) | (12) | (13) | (14) | (15) |
|---|---|---|---|---|---|---|---|---|---|---|---|---|---|---|---|
| (1) Age | – | | | | | | | | | | | | | | |
| (2) Education | .004 | | | | | | | | | | | | | | |
| (3) Husband's SEI | .123 | .383 | | | | | | | | | | | | | |
| (4) Sex-Role Attitudes | .230 | -.276 | -.075 | | | | | | | | | | | | |
| (5) Career Orientation | -.030 | .183 | .082 | -.364 | | | | | | | | | | | |
| (6) Homemaker Orientation | -.011 | -.162 | -.014 | .362 | -.225 | | | | | | | | | | |
| (7) Work Status[b] | .064 | .130 | -.014 | -.242 | .336 | -.140 | | | | | | | | | |
| (8) % Worked All Marriages | -.188 | .171 | .061 | -.279 | .360 | -.119 | .470 | | | | | | | | |
| (9) Fem. Tasks | .071 | -.096 | .057 | .297 | -.118 | .210 | -.220 | -.191 | | | | | | | |
| (10) Masc. Tasks | -.120 | .001 | .040 | -.134 | .016 | .032 | .082 | .038 | .125 | | | | | | |
| (11) Decisions | .050 | .138 | .025 | -.347 | .220 | -.170 | .145 | .117 | -.145 | .019 | | | | | |
| (12) Children Raised | .467 | -.229 | -.149 | .287 | -.214 | .015 | -.115 | -.366 | .069 | -.114 | -.098 | | | | |
| (13) Total Wanted | .107 | -.106 | -.125 | .205 | -.096 | .051 | -.068 | -.084 | -.070 | -.041 | -.101 | .470 | | | |
| (14) Additional Wanted | -.361 | .127 | .029 | -.088 | .121 | .033 | .049 | .283 | -.135 | .074 | .002 | -.544 | .485 | | |
| (15) Boys Wanted – Girls Wanted | .011 | .019 | -.016 | -.026 | -.013 | -.062 | .109 | .003 | -.137 | -.020 | -.003 | .060 | .139 | .073 | – |

[a]For correlations above .15, $p$ <.01.   [b]1 = Not employed, 2 = Employed.

family (percentage of married life employed), sex-role attitudes (i.e., attitudinal traditionalism) and career orientation. The sex-role dimensions most closely related to fertility preferences were sex-role attitude (related to total number of children wanted) and the percentage of married time employed (related to additional children wanted). The high correlations between actual number raised and fertility preferences (.470 for number wanted, $-.542$ for additional wanted) indicate that number raised has an important influence on future preferences. Few people report themselves as wanting a smaller number of children than they already have.

The correlations between background variables and fertility were significant. Education was negatively associated with number of children raised ($-.229$). Age was negatively associated with additional children wanted ($-.361$), but positively associated with number of children raised (.467). In general, the measure of preferences regarding children's sex showed little relationship to either sex-role or demographic variables. Overall, however, Anglo women were slightly more likely to prefer boys to girls ($\overline{X} = .128$, $t = 2.11$, $p<.05$).

The data from Spanish-surnamed women presented in Table 2 show few significant correlations between sex roles and fertility pref-

Table 2. Correlations Between Sex-Role and Fertility Variables for Latinos (N = 136)[a]

|  | (1) | (2) | (3) | (4) | (5) | (6) | (7) | (8) | (9) | (10) | (11) | (12) | (13) | (14) | (15) |
|---|---|---|---|---|---|---|---|---|---|---|---|---|---|---|---|
| (1) Age | – | | | | | | | | | | | | | | |
| (2) Education | -.093 | | | | | | | | | | | | | | |
| (3) Husband's SEI | .051 | .339 | | | | | | | | | | | | | |
| (4) Sex-Role Attitudes | .145 | -.407 | -.124 | | | | | | | | | | | | |
| (5) Career Orientation | .044 | .159 | .080 | -.165 | | | | | | | | | | | |
| (6) Homemaker Orientation | -.038 | -.054 | -.071 | .197 | -.209 | | | | | | | | | | |
| (7) Work Status[b] | .271 | .047 | .015 | -.003 | .254 | -.022 | | | | | | | | | |
| (8) % Worked All Marriages | .078 | .278 | .049 | -.128 | .332 | .024 | .430 | | | | | | | | |
| (9) Fem. Tasks | .019 | -.099 | -.074 | .137 | -.185 | .051 | -.131 | -.154 | | | | | | | |
| (10) Masc. Tasks | .072 | -.122 | .030 | -.012 | -.039 | .047 | -.196 | -.018 | .199 | | | | | | |
| (11) Decisions | .122 | .239 | .036 | -.344 | .091 | .089 | .142 | .192 | -.174 | .090 | | | | | |
| (12) Children Raised | .331 | -.302 | -.077 | .108 | -.144 | .041 | -.044 | -.334 | .065 | .051 | .027 | | | | |
| (13) Total Wanted | .009 | -.080 | .004 | .054 | .016 | .019 | -.014 | -.115 | -.093 | -.022 | -.093 | .398 | | | |
| (14) Additional Wanted | -.330 | .247 | .080 | -.070 | .159 | -.028 | .035 | .253 | -.138 | -.068 | -.098 | -.716 | .356 | | |
| (15) Boys Wanted – Girls Wanted | -.060 | -.053 | -.057 | -.009 | -.009 | -.012 | -.226 | -.040 | -.018 | -.040 | .124 | .093 | .132 | .007 | – |

[a]For correlations above .23, $p$ <.01.          [b]1 = Not employed, 2 = Employed.

erences. However, employment status was significantly negatively related to preferences regarding sex of child, i.e., although there was no overall preference for boys ($\bar{X} = .015$), those who were employed were less likely to prefer boys over girls. Wives who had worked a greater proportion of time during their marriages had raised fewer children, but were more likely to want additional children. In general, however, number of children wanted and number of additional children wanted appeared not to be correlated with sex-role dimensions.

The correlation for blacks presented in Table 3 show that past employment history, and to some extent present employment status, had the most consistent negative relationship to number of children raised. Decision-making within the family (i.e., the wife makes relatively more decisions) was positively related to children raised. These same measures were to some extent related to future fertility preferences for blacks. However, sex-role attitudes also showed a fairly strong relationship to number of children wanted ($r = .409$). Several variables were also related to the measures of preference for boys. High wife participation in both decisions and masculine tasks (and to some extent feminine tasks) was associated with higher preference for boys.

Correlations between the sex role measures and fertility were

Table 3. Correlations Between Sex-Role and Fertility Variables for Blacks (N = 53)[a]

|  | (1) | (2) | (3) | (4) | (5) | (6) | (7) | (8) | (9) | (10) | (11) | (12) | (13) | (14) | (15) |
|---|---|---|---|---|---|---|---|---|---|---|---|---|---|---|---|
| (1) Age | – | | | | | | | | | | | | | | |
| (2) Education | .021 | | | | | | | | | | | | | | |
| (3) Husband's SEI | -.198 | .551 | | | | | | | | | | | | | |
| (4) Sex-Role Attitudes | .269 | -.409 | -.217 | | | | | | | | | | | | |
| (5) Career Orientation | .264 | .174 | .104 | -.194 | | | | | | | | | | | |
| (6) Homemaker Orientation | -.144 | -.113 | -.059 | .108 | -.248 | | | | | | | | | | |
| (7) Work Status[b] | -.105 | .320 | .419 | -.225 | .013 | -.139 | | | | | | | | | |
| (8) % Worked All Marriages | .053 | .357 | .348 | -.212 | .008 | -.403 | .534 | | | | | | | | |
| (9) Fem. Tasks | .088 | -.485 | -.334 | .220 | -.066 | -.002 | -.318 | -.199 | | | | | | | |
| (10) Masc. Tasks | -.119 | -.274 | .040 | -.018 | .194 | -.028 | .011 | -.050 | .035 | | | | | | |
| (11) Decisions | .178 | -.100 | -.238 | .068 | .101 | .181 | -.165 | -.342 | .155 | .227 | | | | | |
| (12) Children Raised | .445 | -.179 | -.107 | .200 | -.025 | .296 | -.247 | -.393 | .098 | .070 | .355 | | | | |
| (13) Total Wanted | .270 | -.148 | -.033 | .409 | -.179 | .247 | -.203 | -.301 | .094 | .140 | .348 | .726 | | | |
| (14) Additional Wanted | -.312 | .077 | .113 | .207 | -.181 | -.134 | .109 | .200 | -.028 | .069 | -.089 | -.557 | .167 | | |
| (15) Boys Wanted – Girls Wanted | .117 | .331 | .201 | -.227 | -.057 | -.199 | .055 | .191 | -.223 | -.345 | -.512 | -.200 | -.269 | -.038 | – |

[a]For correlations above .35, $p < .01$.　　　[b]1 = Not employed, 2 = Employed.

generally somewhat higher for blacks than they were for Anglos. However, data from blacks should be cautiously interpreted because of the small number of blacks in the sample (N = 53). The several significant relationships that are opposite to the expected direction (e.g., higher wife participation in tasks and decisions was associated with preference for boys) also suggest that this ethnic group is in fact different or that these data may not be reliable.

While the correlational analysis suggests the absence of strong relationships between fertility and sex roles, it did find significant relationships between fertility and sex-role traditionalism dimensions of attitudes and role behavior outside the family. While many of the correlations were similar for all three groups, enough differences occurred (e.g., generally lower r's for Latinos, the unexpected relationship between sex-role behaviors in the family and fertility preferences for blacks) that it appears advisable in future research to continue to separately consider the various ethnic groups.

## Causal Analyses

A moderate positive correlation for an ethnic group between (a) sex roles (e.g., attitudes toward women's roles) and (b) fertility and/or fertility preferences might reflect any one of a number of causal patterns. Sex-role variables could influence fertility preferences and present fertility; or sex-role variables and fertility preferences could both be a function of past fertility; or both sets of variables could be spuriously related because they are influenced by one or more other common factors. Similarly, among sex-role variables, various causal analyses could apply. Employment status could influence sex-role attitudes and sex-role behavior within the family; or sex-role attitudes could influence employment status; or sex-role behavior in the family might influence attitudes regarding women's roles.

In order to explore probable causal relationships among variables, the specialized methodology of path analysis described by Duncan (1966), Kerlinger and Pedhazur (1973), and Heise (1969a, 1969b) was employed. Such a method assumes the linearity of relationships and in effect ignores possible interactive relationships. The approach requires the development of a specific causal model delineating relationships among variables. The estimates of causal effect are called path coefficients. It must be remembered that such a structural analysis cannot confirm validity of a particular causal model. Rather, it can disprove a particular model and provide a methodology for estimating the strengths of connections between variables.

Since path analysis becomes exceedingly complex as the number of possible variables increases, the number of variables considered was limited on the basis of the theoretical importance of the variables. Among the sex-role variables, career orientation, employment orientation, and masculine tasks were eliminated. Feminine tasks and decisions were kept because of their theoretical importance as measures of sex-role behavior in the family. Additional children wanted and number of boys minus girls were eliminated as dependent fertility preference variables. Additional children wanted had been created through subtraction of number of children raised from total number of children wanted. Thus, it had common variance with two other variables and could be eliminated. The measure of preference for sex of child was omitted because it was not highly correlated with sex roles. Thus, the 10 variables remaining included three demographic variables (age, education, and husband's socioeconomic status), one measure of fertility (total number of children raised), one measure of role perceptions (attitudes towards women's roles), two measures of sex-role behavior outside of the family (present employment status or percent worked during all marriages),[1] two measures of sex-role behavior in the family (feminine tasks and decisions), and one measure of fertility preferences (total number of children wanted).

Although correlations among variables generally were highest for black women, their number (N = 53) was too small for multivariate analysis. A similar but less severe problem occurred for the Latinos. Thus, the path analysis was limited to the 359 Anglos.

Causal priorities among variables for the theoretical model were determined through the hypotheses outlined in the introduction. These variables stated in causal order of the model are: 1) age, education, and husband's SES, 2) number of children raised (an index of past fertility), 3) attitudes toward women's roles, 4) employment status, 5) feminine tasks and decisions (measures of sex-role behavior in the marital dyad), and 6) total number of children wanted (a measure of fertility preferences).

For purposes of explication, there are no reciprocal causality or feedback loops in the model. Each dependent variable is assumed to be a function of independent variables which have causal priority. Thus, the path coefficients represent standardized partial regression coefficients. Thus, a path analysis procedes through estimation of a series of multiple regression equations.

---

[1] Either present employment status or percent of time worked during all marriages was used in the path analysis. Both variables were not used simultaneously.

Table 4. Standardized Path Coefficients (Full Model)

| Independent Variable | Dependent Variable | | | | | | | |
|---|---|---|---|---|---|---|---|---|
| | 1 | 2 | 3 | 4 | 5 | 6 | 7 | 8 |
| 1. Age | – | .003 | .123 | .491* | .141* | .203* | .026 | -.136* |
| 2. Education | | | .383 | -.175* | -.251* | .072 | -.046 | .039 |
| 3. Husband's Socioeconomic Status | | | | -.146* | .030 | -.118[a] | .086 | -.056 |
| 4. Number of Children Raised | | | | | .174* | -.152* | -.017 | .515* |
| 5. Sex-Role Attitudes | | | | | | -.228* | .248* | .162* |
| 6. Current Employment Status | | | | | | | -.151* | -.016 |
| 7. Feminine Tasks | | | | | | | | -.146* |
| 8. Total Children Wanted | | | | | | | | – |

Note. The path coefficients linking variables 1, 2, and 3 (exogenous variables) are product moment correlations.

[a]Significant at .05 level in full path model, but not significant when education was removed from the regression.

*p <.05.

A full path analysis model (see Table 4) is one in which each variable depends on all prior causal variables.[2] The present model considered regressions based on the causal relationships delineated in the causal hypotheses. However, the full path regressions were also necessary because some causally prior variables may have effects on causally subsequent variables that were not considered in the original hypotheses. If one or more such variable retains significant partial regression coefficients, even after controlling for assumed intervening variables, the model must be respecified to take such a causal link into account.

For Anglos, the analysis proceeded through a number of steps. The procedure first was to compute (a) the regression analyses using only causal variables specified in the hypotheses and (b) the regression analyses using all antecedent variables. Next, instances were identified where the model had been misspecified because (a) causal relationships specified in the hypotheses were not upheld, i.e., the standardized partial regression coefficients based on these causal links were either very small (.05 or less) or not significantly different from zero, or (b) the analysis using all antecedent variables revealed significant causal relationships that had not been specified in the

[2]Decisions was eliminated as a variable at this point because of its lack of relationship with the dependent variable, given the full path model specified.

LINDA J. BECKMAN

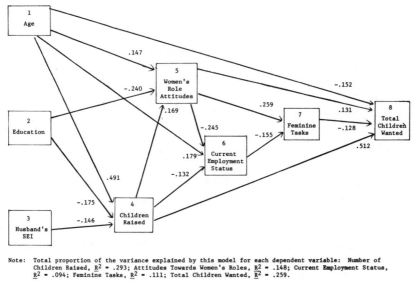

Note: Total proportion of the variance explained by this model for each dependent variable: Number of Children Raised, $R^2$ = .293; Attitudes Towards Women's Roles, $R^2$ = .148; Current Employment Status, $R^2$ = .094; Feminine Tasks, $R^2$ = .111; Total Children Wanted, $\overline{R}^2$ = .259.

FIGURE 1. Path analysis of sex roles and fertility for Anglos.

original hypotheses. Finally, the regressions were again recomputed enlarging or reducing the model to correct for misspecification errors in the hypotheses.

The path diagram in Figure 1 presents the relationships of interest for Anglos. This path model accounted for 26% of the variance in the dependent variable, total children wanted. The model was considered to be plausible because the 25 correlation coefficients between variables could be adequately reproduced using the path diagram. Only one reproduced correlation ($r_{38}$) diverged from the predicted correlations by more than .05 (deviation = .067).

*Sociodemographic Variables.* The three exogenous sociodemographic variables chosen for the present analyses have a variety of direct and indirect effects on fertility and sex roles (Hypothesis 1). While age has a direct negative effect on children wanted ($P_{81} = -.152 = -.152$), it causally operates primarily on this dependent variable through indirect causal links, primarily with number of children raised (.491 × .512 = .251).[3] This, plus a variety of other very small indirect

---

[3]To compute a compound effect, the path coefficients along the causal chain are multiplied together.

effects, leads to a correlation of .107 (see Table 1 for correlations). In contrast to age, education only indirectly affects children wanted ($r_{28}$ = −.106) through its negative effects on number of children raised and attitudes towards women's roles. Husband's socioeconomic index has a moderate negative effect on number of children raised which, in turn, is both indirectly and directly causally linked to total number of children wanted ($r_{28}$ = −.125).

*Number of Children Raised.* The next causal variable in the analysis, number of children raised, mainly has a large direct effect on fertility preferences (i.e., total children wanted), indicated by $P_{84}$ = .512 as compared to a zero-order correlation of .470. However, as suggested in Hypothesis 2a, children raised also has a negative, although fairly small, effect on employment status; number of children raised also positively influences (or at least is related to) present attitudes toward women's roles (Hypothesis 2b). Also of interest is the predicted lack of direct relationship between children raised and role behavior within the family (Hypothesis 2c).

*Sex-Role Variables.* Traditionalism in attitudes toward women's roles negatively affected employment status ($P_{65}$ = −.245) and positively affected wife's relative performance of feminine tasks ($P_{75}$ = .259), thus offering support for Hypothesis 3. As also was predicted (Hypothesis 4), being employed had a negative effect on wife's relative performance of feminine tasks (i.e., employed women's task behavior was less sex-role stereotyped or traditional).

*Total Number of Children Wanted.* A most important consideration is the effects of these sex-role (and other) variables on total number of children wanted. As can be seen, although division of decision making in the marital dyad has no effect on total children wanted, as initially predicted in Hypothesis 5 one dimension of sex-role behaviors within the dyad (i.e., feminine tasks) did show a moderate influence on children wanted. In contrast to our prediction that non-traditional behavior (i.e., lesser wife participation in feminine tasks) would be negatively associated with fertility preferences, the opposite occurred. Women who performed a greater proportion of the feminine tasks (as compared to their husbands) wanted *fewer* children. This is indicated by the significant negative path coefficient ($P_{87}$ = −.128). It might be thought that this finding occurred because these women already had more children, but this negative path coefficient remained after the effects of number of children raised had been controlled in the regression of total number of children wanted.[4]

Attitudes toward women's roles (i.e., traditionalism), as was predicted (Hypothesis 4), had a moderate direct positive effect on total children wanted ($P_{85} = .131$), but interestingly enough, also had a small indirect causal link ($.259 \times [-.128] = -.033$) that operated through feminine tasks and was negative. In addition, part of the correlation between these two variables ($r_{58} = .205$) is due to common antecedent factors such as number of children raised. (The two other variables directly affecting total children wanted were, as previously stated, number of children raised, which had the largest path coefficient [$P_{84} = .512$], and age, which negatively influenced total children wanted [$P_{81} = -.152$].)

While employment status did not directly affect total children wanted, it showed a small indirect effect through feminine tasks ($[-.155] \times [-.128] = .020$). However, overall there was a low negative correlation coefficient between employment status and total children wanted ($r_{68} = -.068$) because of the common (but opposite in direction) effects of age, attitudes toward women's roles, children raised, and education on both variables.[5]

In summary, feminine tasks and sex-role attitudes both showed significant causal influences upon fertility preferences even when the effects of past fertility (i.e., children raised) and demographic variables were controlled (as they were in the regression of total children wanted on all seven antecedent variables in Table 4). However, these effects, although significant ($p < .05$), were fairly small. With these two sex-role variables included, .259 of the variance in the final reduced path model regression of total children wanted was explained; without these two variables, the proportion of variance explained was .237.

## DISCUSSION

The correlational data suggest that the relationship between sex roles and fertility is subtle at best. For Anglos and blacks sex-role

---

[4]A standardized partial regression coefficient indicates the effect of a variable on a dependent variable when the effects of all other variables in that regression equation have been controlled. In this case for the final reduced form of the path analysis, children wanted was regressed on feminine tasks, children raised, age, and traditionalism.

[5]When percent worked during all marriages was substituted for current work status (as Variable 6 in Figure 1) the proportion of variance explained in Work Status ($R^2 = .166$) and Children Wanted ($R^2 = .267$) increased slightly for the reduced path model of Figure 1.

attitudes do appear to be more highly associated with children raised and fertility preferences than does division of tasks and decisions within the household. Past and present employment experience (i.e., role behavior outside of the family) also were related to fertility and fertility preferences for all three groups. However, preferences for children of a particular sex appeared generally unrelated to sex-role variables of the study. While two of three sociodemographic variables included showed substantial relationship to number of children raised, these demographic factors were generally unrelated to total number of children wanted. The findings also support our assumption that separate consideration of the relationship between fertility and other variables is warranted for each ethnic group.

The path analysis approach which was applied only for Anglos suggested that number of children raised has the largest direct effect on total children wanted. Age also showed a direct negative effect on total children wanted. Even when the effects of children raised and demographic variables were controlled, however, *attitudes* toward women's roles and sex-role *behaviors* in the marital dyad still had direct effects on total number of children wanted. Attitudes toward women's roles affected fertility desires both directly and through their indirect effects on employment status and feminine tasks. Women more traditional in their sex-role attitudes desired more children. However, women who performed a greater proportion of feminine tasks in the household, and by standard definitions of sex role thereby reflect a traditional pattern, actually desired fewer rather than more children. This may have occurred because more children only add to the work that a woman has to do, particularly a woman with primary responsibility for household tasks. Thus, despite the moderate positive correlation between sex-role attitudes and sex-role behavior in the family ($r = .297$), these two variables had opposite effects on number of children wanted.

Also of interest was the interrelationship among sex-role variables. Role behavior outside the family (i.e., employment status) appears to affect relative performance of feminine tasks in the dyad (and, thus, fertility desired). As found in past studies of the effects of female employment (e.g., Heer, 1963; Scanzoni, 1970), current employment is associated with less performance of feminine tasks (relative to husband) and less traditional sex-role attitudes. The employed woman may have less time for household tasks and more money to hire household help.

One of the aims of this research was to investigate the effects of fertility on sex roles as well as vice versa. It was hypothesized that the number of children one already has can affect sex roles. The path analysis indicates that this may indeed be the case. However, in the variables studied apparently present number of children only directly affects role options outside of the family and sex-role attitudes. Its effects on role behavior within the family appear to operate indirectly through its effects on extra-family role behaviors (i.e., employment status) and on attitudes toward women's roles. For Anglos, the correlation between number of children and the sex-role variables of employment status and role attitudes may be, in part, due to the common influences of demographic factors on both sets of factors. For instance, persons of a particular educational level or socioeconomic status may have certain normative beliefs or behavior patterns regarding both fertility and women's roles. However, the present results confirm that these correlations are due to something more than spurious relationships caused by these antecedent factors. Even when the effects of the three key demographic variables are controlled, total number of children raised has an independent effect on sex-role variables.

The model specified in Figure 1 has its limitations. Employment status and traditionalism in sex-role attitudes may influence number of children rather than the opposite. All that is claimed in the present analysis is that the data are consistent with the opposite interpretation presented in Figure 1. It remains for further research using nonrecursive models (i.e., those with reciprocal causality) to clarify these interrelationships.

In conclusion, these results indicate that, at least for Anglos, number of children raised may influence sex role behavior and attitudes which, in turn, may be part of a complex of factors which partially determine current fertility desires. Such findings suggest that it is valuable to consider sex-role and other psychological variables as well as sociodemographic variables when trying to understand fertility desires. Most importantly, the various dimensions of sex roles may influence fertility desires in opposite ways, as indicated by the positive effect of traditionalism of attitudes and negative effect of relative performance of feminine tasks on total children desired. The one variable with the largest influence on fertility desires is the number of children that one already has. However, even when the effects of sociodemographic variables and current number of children are controlled, sex-role variables are related to fertility desires.

## REFERENCES

Beckman, L. J. The relative rewards and costs of parenthood and employment for employed women. *Psychology of Women Quarterly*, 1978, 2, 215-234.

Beckman, L. J., & Houser, B. B. The more you have, the more you do: The relationship between wife's employment, sex-role attitudes and household behavior. *Psychology of Women Quarterly*, in press.

Blood, R. O., & Wolfe, D. M. *Husbands and wives*. New York: Free Press, 1960.

Duncan, O. D. Path analysis: Sociological examples. *American Journal of Sociology*, 1966, *72*, 1–16.

Fox, G. L. Sex-role attitudes as predictors of contraceptive use among unmarried university students. *Sex Roles*, 1977, *3*, 265–283.

Haas, P. Maternal role incompatibility and fertility in Latin America. *Journal of Social Issues*, 1972, *28*, 111–128.

Havro-Mannila, E. The position of Finnish women: Regional and cross-national comparisons. *Journal of Marriage and the Family*, 1969, *31*, 339–347.

Heer, D. M. The measurement and bases of family power: An overview. *Marriage and Family Living*, 1963, *25*, 133–139.

Heise, D. R. Separating reliability and stability in test-retest correlation. *American Sociological Review*, 1969, *34*, 93–101. (a)

Heise, D. R. Problems in path analysis and causal inference. In E. F. Borgatta (Ed.), *Sociological methodology 1969*. San Francisco: Jossey-Bass, 1969. (b)

Houser, B. B., & Beckman, L. J. Background characteristics and women's dual-role attitudes. *Sex Roles*, in press.

Kerlinger, F. N., & Pedhazur, E. J. *Multiple regression in behavioral research*. New York: Holt, Rinehart & Winston, 1973.

Mason, K. O., & Bumpass, L. L. U.S. women's sex role ideology, 1970. *American Journal of Sociology*, 1975, *80*, 1212–1219.

Ryder, N. B., & Westoff, C. F. *Reproduction in the United States: 1965*. Princeton: Princeton University Press, 1971.

Scanzoni, J. Gender roles and the process of fertility control. *Journal of Marriage and the Family*, 1976, *38*, 677–691.

Scanzoni, J. *Opportunity and the family*. New York: Free Press, 1970.

Scanzoni, J. *Sex roles, life styles, and childbearing*. New York: Free Press, 1975.

Siegel, A. E., & Haas, M. B. The working mother: A review of research . *Child Development*, 1963, *34*, 513–542.

Spence, J. T., & Helmreich, R. The attitudes toward women scale: An objective instrument to measure attitudes toward the rights and roles of women in contemporary society. (Ms. No. 153) *Journal Supplement Abstract Service Catalog of Selected Documents in Psychology*, 1972, *2*, 66–67.

Tangri, S. S. Determinants of occupational role innovation among college women. *Journal of Social Issues*, 1972, *28*, 177–200.

Terry, G. B. Rival explanations in the work-fertility relationship. *Population Studies*, 1975, *29*, 191–205.

Turner, J., & Simmons, A. B. Sex roles and fertility: Which influences which? *Canadian Studies in Population*, in press.

# Fertility, Sex Role Attitudes, and Labor Force Participation

Arland Thornton and Donald Camburn

*The University of Michigan*

Data from the 1970 National Fertility Study were used to investigate the relationships between sex role attitudes and the childbearing and labor force participation of women. While several relevant dimensions of sex role attitudes were identified, it was found that the most crucial aspect for working and fertility was the extent to which the woman identified the female role as that of housewife and homemaker. Those having traditional definitions concerning this role were less likely to be working, and had fewer plans to work in the future. In addition, as expected, women with traditional sex role definitions had more children than others. While the orientation of the woman toward the home was the primary correlate of work and fertility, those who felt that women had little control over their lives had higher fertility than others—a relationship which could be explained partially, but not entirely, in terms of unplanned childbearing.

Postwar America has been characterized by rapid social change, including important changes in the structure and organization of families. There has been a transformation in the values and attitudes of women toward traditional sex roles, toward the place of women in the structure of the family, and toward the position of women in society in general (Mason, Czajka, & Arber, 1976). An important social movement has developed that attempts to maximize opportun-

---

The authors wish to express appreciation to Richard Curtin, Gerald Garin, Toby Epstein Jayaratne, Graham Staines, and Burkhard Strumpel for their helpful suggestions and comments during various stages of the research. The data upon which this publication is based were collected pursuant to Contract #PH-43-65-1048 with the National Institutes of Health, Public Health Service, Department of Health, Education, and Welfare with Norman B. Ryder and Charles F. Westoff being the principal investigators.

*Psychology of Women Quarterly, Vol. 4(1) Fall 1979*
0361-6843/79/1500-0061$00.95 © 1979 Human Sciences Press

ities for women in society and improve their status. Record numbers of women have left the traditional "housewife" role to participate in paid employment and make substantial contributions to family finances and social status (Oppenheimer, 1977). This rise in female employment has been paralleled by a dramatic drop in birth rates following the postwar "baby boom."

The research reported in this paper was motivated by the hypothesis that sex role attitudes and the ideas people have about acceptable role definitions for women are related to fertility. Sex role orientations could affect fertility directly by modifying desired family size or by influencing the effectiveness of contraception. It is also possible that sex role attitudes could influence labor force participation plans and experience which, in turn, affect fertility. While the two mechanisms just mentioned posit a causal influence of sex role attitudes on fertility and labor force participation, it is also likely that both fertility and female employment affect sex role attitudes. In this paper several aspects of the interrelationships between sex role attitudes, labor force participation, and fertility are investigated.

## METHOD

### Subjects

The data used in this analysis, the 1970 National Fertility Study, were obtained from a national probability sample of ever-married women under 45 years old who were asked about their fertility and work histories, their future childbearing and work intentions, and their attitudes concerning several sex roles issues (Westoff & Ryder, 1977). The analysis was limited to currently married women to eliminate the effects of marital status.

### Procedure

*Sex Role Indices.* Respondents were asked a series of 18 questions designed to determine their attitudes towards various roles of women in society and in the home. These questions can be found in Figure 2. Possible responses ranged from "strongly agree" to "strongly disagree" and were ordered on a five point scale ("undecided" and "don't know" responses were assigned a value of three). Where necessary, categories were reordered for analysis so that for all questions a *low score indicates an egalitarian or non-traditional response.*

The correlations among the sex role items exhibited a relationship among several measures which were expected to cluster on theoretical

## ARLAND THORNTON AND DONALD CAMBURN

TABLE 1

Zero Order Correlations of Women's Sex Role Attitude Measures: 1970 National Fertility Survey

| Sex Role Measures | 1 | 2 | 3 | 4 | 5 | 6 | 7 | 8 | 9 | 10 | 11 | 12 | 13 | 14 | 15 | 16 | 17 |
|---|---|---|---|---|---|---|---|---|---|---|---|---|---|---|---|---|---|
| 1 - Men Can Plan-Women Cannot | | | | | | | | | | | | | | | | | |
| 2 - Mother Work-Child Hurt | .10 | | | | | | | | | | | | | | | | |
| 3 - Relations/Working Mother | .07 | .52 | | | | | | | | | | | | | | | |
| 4 - Men Should Work-Women Should Not | .14 | .42 | .40 | | | | | | | | | | | | | | |
| 5 - Men-Women Equal Opportunities | .06 | .07 | .15 | .14 | | | | | | | | | | | | | |
| 6 - Men Should Share Housework | .00 | .14 | .17 | .17 | .19 | | | | | | | | | | | | |
| 7 - Women Career | .04 | .25 | .27 | .24 | .23 | .18 | | | | | | | | | | | |
| 8 - Men Should Not Work Under Women | .03 | .04 | .11 | .09 | .24 | .13 | .20 | | | | | | | | | | |
| 9 - Women Happiest at Home | .14 | .31 | .34 | .43 | .20 | .16 | .26 | .14 | | | | | | | | | |
| 10 - Girls-Boys | .06 | .08 | .11 | .14 | .22 | .14 | .13 | .10 | .11 | | | | | | | | |
| 11 - Men-Women Equal Pay for Equal Jobs | .05 | .00 | .09 | .05 | .34 | .15 | .11 | .19 | .11 | .13 | | | | | | | |
| 12 - Women Executives? | .04 | .11 | .16 | .19 | .42 | .20 | .22 | .20 | .21 | .23 | .25 | | | | | | |
| 13 - Working Women Guilty | .17 | .30 | .31 | .32 | .13 | .10 | .21 | .10 | .35 | .10 | .05 | .12 | | | | | |
| 14 - Have Baby-Still Keep Job | -.04 | .13 | .11 | .08 | .16 | .15 | .14 | .07 | .03 | .08 | .14 | .15 | .04 | | | | |
| 15 - Big Families Happy | .15 | .11 | .14 | .18 | .14 | .00 | .10 | .08 | .26 | .06 | .07 | .13 | .21 | -.03 | | | |
| 16 - Libbers are Misfits | .00 | .13 | .10 | .14 | .12 | .07 | .09 | .04 | .10 | .09 | .02 | .15 | .12 | .08 | .09 | | |
| 17 - Child Care Centers? | -.08 | .09 | .09 | .09 | .19 | .14 | .13 | .09 | .02 | .08 | .12 | .18 | -.03 | .26 | -.02 | .11 | |
| 18 - Sex Exists for Men? | .21 | .00 | .06 | .03 | .06 | -.05 | .02 | .06 | .12 | .00 | .10 | .01 | .17 | -.09 | .18 | .01 | -.09 |

Note:  All items are scaled so that 1 = egalitarian response and 5 = traditional response.  Sample is all
currently married women less than 45 years old, N = 5,981.

grounds (Table 1). Those items, which asked about home related attitudes showed moderate positive intercorrelations.[1] Items which relate to equality outside the home also demonstrated positive correlations.

In order to construct summary indices, factor analysis was conducted (see Table 2 for the factor loadings). Three factors were extracted using oblique rotations (orthogonal rotations were also computed and similar results obtained). Variables loading at .30 or more were considered for inclusion in indices. In interpreting the results of the factor analysis, however, theoretical considerations took precedence in determining the sensibility of the factors that were extracted.

Five items demonstrated strong correlations with the first factor extracted ("Mother work-child hurt"; "Relations/working mother"; "Men should work, women should not"; "Women happiest at home"; and "Working women guilty"). These items align theoretically, as all measured, to

[1]Although the intercorrelations between these items were reported by Mason and Bumpass (1975), they are repeated here for several reasons: the sample used in our analysis included only *currently* married women while Mason and Bumpass used the entire sample of *ever* married women; personal communications with the authors indicate that their table of correlations (p. 214) had several labels interchanged during transcription; and that although a footnote in the article indicated the direction of response categories was reordered so that a low score indicated a traditional attitude, it appears that this was not done and the signs of the coefficients reported do not necessarily reflect the true relationship.

PSYCHOLOGY OF WOMEN QUARTERLY

TABLE 2

Women's Sex Role Attitude Measures: Primary Factor Loadings
1970 National Fertility Study

| | Factor 1 | Factor 2 | Factor 3 |
|---|---|---|---|
| 1 - Men Can Plan-Women Cannot | .104 | .029 | .346 |
| 2 - Mother Work-Child Hurt | .756 | -.137 | -.062 |
| 3 - Relations/Working Mother | .657 | .008 | .024 |
| 4 - Men Should Work-Women Should Not | .613 | .036 | .091 |
| 5 - Men-Women Equal | -.056 | .699 | .054 |
| 6 - Men Should Share Housework | .176 | .274 | -.140 |
| 7 - Women Career | .308 | .254 | .003 |
| 8 - Men Should Not Work Under Women | .009 | .349 | .067 |
| 9 - Women Happiest at Home | .482 | .129 | .264 |
| 10 - Girls-Boys | .052 | .302 | .013 |
| 11 - Men-Women Equal Pay for Equal Jobs | -.103 | .495 | .065 |
| 12 - Women Executives? | .038 | .585 | .005 |
| 13 - Working Women Guilty | .448 | .024 | .297 |
| 14 - Have Baby-Still Keep Job | .116 | .261 | -.267 |
| 15 - Big Families Happy | .145 | .121 | .359 |
| 16 - Libbers and Misfits | .152 | .126 | -.015 |
| 17 - Child Care Centers? | .069 | .304 | .296 |
| 18 - Sex Exists for Men? | -.002 | .067 | .443 |

Factor loadings are from an oblique rotation. See Table 1, Appendix
A for the exact wording of the questions.

some degree, the extent to which women viewed their proper role as being homemakers and the extent to which outside activity was thought to create difficulty in the home. These five items were combined additively and the resulting index was labelled *Home Orientation,* indicating that women scoring high on this dimension believed that a homemaking role was valuable and that they would receive satisfaction from such a role.

Five variables correlated with the second factor, but four of these had somewhat stronger correlations and were very similar in the theoretical dimension they measured: equality of the sexes in the labor force. Because "Child care centers" was bi-factor, correlating with both factors 2 and 3, it was excluded from this summary index. The remaining four questions, "Men-women equal opportunities," "Men should not work under women," "Men-women equal pay," and "Women executives," were added and the resulting index was labelled *Job Prerogatives for Men,* indicating the extent to which the respondent felt men should have more opportunities for jobs, more prestigious jobs, and more income than women.

Although the third factor correlated with four items, "Child care centers" was bi-factor and was excluded for that reason. "Big families happy" was eliminated because it is a fertility variable, and inclusion of a measure of fertility norms in an index of sex role attitudes would have entered it directly on both sides of the equation in models of fertility. The remaining two items, "Men can plan, women cannot" and "Sex exists for

ARLAND THORNTON AND DONALD CAMBURN

men," were scaled as *Women Passive;* women scoring high on this index were assumed to view the world as being more easily manipulated by men and as being more for male enjoyment than female.

The final summary index was created primarily, though not entirely, on theoretical grounds. Two sex role questions, "Child care centers" and "Have baby-keep job" ascertained attitudes towards special social accommodations making it easier and more rewarding for women to have dual careers, both as mothers and as participants in the labor force. There was a correlation between these items ($r = +.26$), although factor analysis showed no underlying structure with which these variables related. Based on the similar and fairly unique theoretical character of these two items, as well as their intercorrelation, they were added and labelled as *Opposed Special Privileges,* indicating that women who scored high on this dimension were opposed to societal accomodations for women as working mothers.

*Labor Force Participation.* The 1970 National Fertility Study asked a series of questions concerning participation in the labor force as well as future plans for work. Women who were working were asked why they were working, and women who were not working but planned to look for work in the future were asked about the circumstances under which they would look for employment. Shown in Figure 1 is the exact wording of these questions, the branching pattern of the interview schedule, and the distribution of the women across the seven categories defined by the questions.

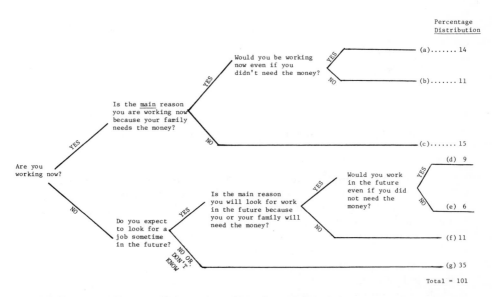

FIGURE 1. Questions and format used to obtain labor force participation, future work plans, and reasons for working, 1970 National Fertility Study.

1. A man can make long range plans for his life, but a woman has to take things as they come. (Do you strongly agree, agree, disagree, or strongly disagree?)

2. A pre-school child is likely to suffer if his mother works.

3. A working mother can establish just as warm and secure a relationship with her children as a mother who does not work.

4. It is much better for everyone involved if the man is the achiever outside the home and the woman takes care of the home and family.

5. A woman should have exactly the same job opportunities as a man.

6. Men should share the work around the house with women such as doing dishes, cleaning, and so forth.

7. A woman should not let bearing and rearing children stand in the way of a career if she wants it.

8. On the job, men should not refuse to work under women.

9. Women are much happier if they stay at home and take care of their children.

10. Young girls are entitled to as much independence as young boys.

11. Men and women should be paid the same money if they do the same work.

12. Women should be considered as seriously as men for jobs as executives or politicians or even President.

13. If anything happened to one of the children while the mother was working, she could never forgive herself.

14. A woman's job should be kept for her when she is having a baby.

15. You usually find the happiest families are those with a large number of children.

16. Many of those in women's rights organizations today seem to be unhappy misfits.

17. There should be free child-care centers so that women could take jobs.

18. Sex seems to exist mainly for the man's pleasure.

FIGURE 2. Sex role questions, 1970 National Fertility Study.

In order to use these data to investigate the relationships existing between sex role ideology, fertility, and labor force orientation, the categories in Figure 1 were combined in various ways to form three separate dichotomous variables. *Working Now* (a–c) measured current work status only, and ignored future intentions and reasons for working. The second variable, *Work Now or Future,* scored all who were working or would work in the future (a–f) as one, while all other (group g) were scored zero. A third variable, called *Work Commitment,* scored women who were working (or would work) for noneconomic reasons, or would work even if they did not need the money, as one, and all other women as zero. This variable measured the respondent's commitment to, and identification with, employment.

*Fertility.* Three measures of fertility were used. The first, current parity, indicated the number of children a woman had ever borne by the time of the interview. The second fertility variable used was the number of children a woman intended to have *in addition* to those she already had. The last fertility variable, the total intended number of children, is the number of children a woman intended to have by the time her childbearing was complete.

## Causal Interrelationships

The following paragraphs examine the possible causal mechanisms that could produce interrelationships between each of the four sex role attitudes and female employment and fertility:

*Home Orientation.* Existing research suggests that home orientation is positively related to family size. (Bumpass, 1974; Clarkson, Vogel, Broverman, & Broverman, 1970; Goldberg, 1974, 1975; Hoffman & Wyatt, 1960; Rainwater, 1965; Scanzoni, 1975; Waite & Stolzenberg, 1976). There are several causal mechanisms that could produce a positive relationship between home orientation and family size. First, women with this orientation are likely to accept and value the traditional role definition of wife as including motherhood and the rearing of children. Since this definition of the adult female role includes children, it is unlikely that such a woman would be voluntarily childless. In addition, familial relationships are probably a primary source of satisfaction and happiness for a woman with high home orientation: this might provide an impetus for having several children rather than few.

A second possible mechanism producing a positive relationship between home orientation and childbearing is indirect, involving female labor force participation. Women who score high on *Home Orientation* accept the traditional home role for women and believe that deviation from it could produce negative effects. It seems reasonable to expect that to the extent women found contentment and accomplishment from the homemaking role, they would not be motivated to look elsewhere for fulfillment. Therefore, the desire to work might be less for them than for others. Furthermore, while the causal mechanisms producing the relationship between labor force participation and fertility is not well understood, the negative correlation between these two variables is well established. Thus, to the extent that home orientation decreases participation in the labor force, it would probably increase fertility.

It is also possible that women with many children and the necessity of spending considerable amounts of time caring for them would feel a need to make their attitudes consistent with their behavior. As a result, their large families could cause them to move in the direction of having greater home orientation. Similarly, women who are committed to work and who view paid employment as satisfying are likely to have fewer children and are likely to move towards the less traditional end of the home orientation scale.

*Women Passive.*   If was hypothesized that *Women Passive* would be related positively with childbearing: women scoring high on this variable would have more children than others. Indeed, the factor analysis showed that this dimension was closely related to the question concerning the happiest families being those with a large number of children (Table 2). Also, women who were high on this variable would be more accepting of the conditions and constraints placed upon them by children and it is likely they would be more prone "to take things as they come." Therefore, it may be that these people have more children both because they want more and because they are less active in planning their lives and less efficient and persistent in effecting plans.

A second reason for expecting a positive association between *Women Passive* and childbearing is that those who experience unplanned and possibly unwanted fertility may see life in different terms than those who have been efficient planners. That is, unplanned fertility may cause women to feel that they cannot make and carry out plans. Since the bulk of child care responsibilities falls on women, it is likely that unplanned children would affect the attitudes of women toward planning more than they would affect the attitudes of men. Since the burden of unplanned childbearing falls more heavily on wives, it also may be true that unplanned childbearing influences the feelings of women toward sex, causing them to see sex as existing more for men than women.

In addition, women scoring high on *Women Passive* may be less active in planning careers and obtaining satisfaction from participation in the labor force, traditionally a masculine endeavor. These women, therefore, would be less likely to actually be working and would be less committed to work. It would be expected, therefore, that women scoring high on *Women Passive* would have higher fertility because of their low involvement with work.

*Job Prerogatives for Men.*   It seems unlikely that this dimension would influence family size directly, but it is possible that fertility behavior and plans would influence this variable. Research has shown that family size and the age of the youngest child are related to labor force participation; those with more children and with younger children are less likely to work than others. Since these women are less likely to work, their economic fortunes are more clearly tied to the success of their husbands than are the circumstances of other wives. To the extent that these women's economic circumstances are tied to their husbands' incomes, they would tend to view equal opportunity as disadvantageous because equality in the labor force for women could reduce the opportunity and rewards for their husbands, thereby materially hurting themselves. Therefore, simple self-interest could produce a positive association between fertility and *Job Prerogatives for Men.*

Several factors could produce a negative association between *Job Prerogatives for Men* and labor force participation. First, those who think men should have more opportunities and rewards would probably view the work world as less hospitable for women than for others. Therefore, it is unlikely that they would see the labor force as an attractive place for satisfying their own needs. Secondly, women who desire to work and those who are actually working may have more reasons to be unhappy with unequal opportunity. They are desirous of·obtaining the most from their actual or desired activity and probably see unequal arrangements as hindering them. For these women, personal and direct rewards would result from equality. Finally, working is likely to provide access to ideologies advocating equality. This exposure is likely to decrease agreement with the notion that social inequality is acceptable. To the extent that these mechanisms are operative and to the extent that fertility and work are negatively related, one would expect a positive association between fertility and *Job Prerogatives for Men.*

*Opposed Special Privileges.* It is difficult to predict the relationship between *Opposed Special Privileges* and childbearing. Those with many children or who plan large families would need day care centers and employment continuity more than those with smaller families, in order to lessen the costs of employment. These women would also be unhappy about losing seniority and job continuity if they were to quit work to have a baby. But they only need the childcare mechanisms if they are also desirous of working. That is, women who do not intend to work have virtually no need to be concerned about the issues making up this index. However, the fertility of women who actually work or plan to work would be expected to be lower. On the one hand, one mechanism would predict higher fertility and on the other hand, there is a mechanism which would reduce childbearing. Therefore, our analysis of the association between *Opposed Special Privileges* and childbearing did not include the element of hypothesis testing; it only described the relationship observed.

# RESULTS

The statistical analysis was complicated by the complexity of the causal mechanisms operating. Part of the relationship between sex role attitudes and fertility could be produced by sex role attitudes influencing fertility directly, while some of the relationship could be produced by sex role attitudes affecting labor force attachment, which, in turn, influences fertility. There is also the possibility of causal influence going from labor force participation and fertility to sex role attitudes. Furthermore, the causal structures hypothesized for the four sex role attitude dimensions are not identical. Additionally, there is the possibility of reciprocal causation between labor force participation and fertility. We believe that the type of methodological sophistication required to estimate the precise causal effects in such a complex structural equations model would outrun both our theoretical knowledge and the quality of the available data, as well as tremendously complicate the presentation of results. Therefore, to reduce the complexity of the analysis, a simpler analytical model was used, which assumed that sex role attitudes influenced labor force participation, and that both labor force participation and sex role attitudes influenced fertility. Causal forces from fertility to work and from fertility and work to sex role attitudes were assumed not to exist. Therefore, in interpreting the data, the nature of the simplifying assumptions should be kept clearly in mind. While the coefficients that are presented clearly imply causation in one direction only, it should be remembered that they could be the result of reciprocal causation or causation in the opposite direction to that implied by the structure of the analysis. The coefficients should be interpreted in the relational, rather than the causal sense.

The analysis proceeded in three stages. The first stage investigated the overall relationship between sex role attitudes and fertility with no attempt to decompose the total effect into the part that went directly from sex roles to fertility and the part that went indirectly from sex roles to fertility through labor force participation. The second stage of the analysis considered labor force participation by examining the relationship between female employment and sex role attitudes. This stage of the analysis permitted the investigation of the hypothesis that sex role attitudes could influence fertility through their impact on female employment. Finally, the third stage investigated the impact of sex role attitudes on fertility *net* of labor force participation. Thus the third stage allowed the estimation of the part of the relationship between sex roles and fertility that operates independently of labor force participation.

It is, of course, difficult to evaluate relationships without taking into account other variables and forces operating. Fertility behavior and expectations are influenced by demographic and social factors which also are related to sex role attitudes and labor force participation. Failure to take these other forces into account would bias the relationships observed. For this reason, multivariate analysis (ordinary least squares regression) was conducted, which permitted the influence of the other variables to be taken into account.

*Sex Roles and Fertility.* The multivariate analysis proceeded in steps. Age, religion and race, which are causally *prior* to both sex roles and childbearing, were controlled in the first step, referred to as Model 1. Then stricter conditions were introduced by including var-

ARLAND THORNTON AND DONALD CAMBURN

Table 3

Zero Order Correlations between Fertility, Labor Force Variables, Sex Role
Attitudes, and Background Variables: 1970 National Fertility Study

| | Current Parity | Additional Intended | Total Intended | Working Now | Work Now or Future | Work Commitment |
|---|---|---|---|---|---|---|
| Home Orientation | .09* | .03* | .12* | -.26* | -.28* | -.30* |
| Job Prerogatives for Men | .09* | -.04* | .08* | -.01 | -.09* | -.10* |
| Opposed Special Privileges | .00 | -.02* | -.02 | -.03* | -.10* | -.06* |
| Women Passive | .12* | -.07* | .09* | -.03* | .00 | -.04* |
| Age | .45* | -.56* | .15* | .08* | -.07* | -.07* |
| Age at Marriage | -.20* | .06* | -.19* | -.03* | .01 | -.06* |
| Religion (Catholic=1), Other=0) | .08* | .08* | .14* | -.06* | -.02* | -.02 |
| Race (White=0, Other=1) | .12* | .01 | .14* | .04* | .09* | .06* |
| Education | -.24* | .12* | -.19* | .09* | .09* | .17* |
| Husband's Income | .08* | -.25* | -.07* | -.10* | -.13* | .03* |
| Working Now | -.09* | .02 | -.09* | - | .59* | .39* |
| Work Now or Future | -.11* | .06* | -.08* | - | - | .70* |
| Work Commitment | -.16* | .08* | -.13* | - | - | - |
| Current Parity | - | -.47* | .83* | | | |
| Additional Intended | - | - | .11* | | | |

N=5,981

*Coefficient is at least two times its standard error. Standard errors were estimated on the assumption
of simple random sampling and did not include the design effects resulting from the use of a complex sample
design in the 1970 NFS.

iables which are possibly causally prior to sex role attitudes and
fertility, but which may also be affected by them. The three variables
added in this step (Model 2) were education, age at marriage, and
husband's income. Thus, the Model 2 analysis permitted estimation
of the relationships between sex roles and fertility net of the other six
variables. It should be stressed that the net effects in Model 2 may be
less than the total, since some of the overall influence may operate
through the control variables. Note that when additional children
intended was analyzed, the number already born was controlled.
This was necessary because of the very strong dependence of future
fertility on the present number. The zero order correlations between
sex role attitudes and fertility and work, as well as the correlations
between fertility, work, and the other variables used in the multivariate analysis, are shown in Table 3.

The first stage analysis, which related sex role attitudes to fertility
and ignored the role of labor force participation, is summarized in
Table 4, where the standardized regression coefficients for the sex
role variables are reported. The first coefficients were obtained by
adding the sex role variables one at a time to the basic models (upper

PSYCHOLOGY OF WOMEN QUARTERLY

TABLE 4

Multivariate Analysis of the Relationship between Current Parity,
Additional Intended Children, Total Intended Children, and
Sex Role Attitudes:  1970 National Fertility Study

| | Current Parity | | Additional Intended Children | | Total Intended Children | |
|---|---|---|---|---|---|---|
| | Model 1 | Model 2 | Model 1 | Model 2 | Model 1 | Model 2 |
| Variables Entered One at a Time | | | | | | |
| Home Orientation | .08* | .04* | .06* | .07* | .12* | .08* |
| Job Prerogatives for Men | .08* | .02 | .00 | .01 | .08* | .03* |
| Opposed Special Privileges | .00 | .00 | .01 | .01 | .00 | .01 |
| Women Passive | .08* | .04* | -.02* | -.02* | .06* | .03* |
| Variables Entered Together | | | | | | |
| Home Orientation | .06* | .03* | .07* | .08* | .10* | .08* |
| Job Prerogatives for Men | .06* | .02 | -.01 | .00 | .05* | .02 |
| Opposed Special Privileges | -.02 | -.01 | -.01 | .00 | -.02 | -.01 |
| Women Passive | .06* | .04* | -.03 | -.03* | .04* | .02 |

Note.  In all cases Model 1 controlled age, religion, and race.  To these
Model 1 controls, Model 2 added age at marriage, education, and husband's
income.  For the analysis of additional intended children, all models also included a control for the number of children already born.  The first
set of coefficients was obtained by separately including each sex role
ideology variable in separate regression equations.  The second set of coefficients was obtained by entering all four variables into the same regression equation.

*Coefficient is at least two times its standard error.  Standard
errors were estimated on the assumption of simple random sampling, and did
not include the design effects resulting from the use of a complex sample
design in the 1970 NFS.

Figures listed are standardized regression coefficients, N = 5981.

panels of Table 4). Thus, the relationship for each role dimension can
be seen with only the basic set of variables controlled. The second set
of coefficients was obtained by adding all four sex role variables
*simultaneously* to the basic models (lower panels of Table 4). Thus,
these coefficients were estimated controlling the effects of the other
role variables in addition to the basic controls.

When the sex roles variables were entered into the basic models
of fertility one at a time, the coefficients for *Home Orientation* were
generally consistent with our hypotheses. For all three dependent
variables, the coefficients for *Home Orientation* were positive in
Model 1. The coefficients remained positive and statistically significant with Model 2 (Table 4) indicating that there was indeed a relationship net of the other factors in those models. However, the introduction of Model 2 controls reduced the coefficients somewhat.

*Job Prerogatives for Men* was positively related to current parity and to total intended children in Model 1, but the Model 2 controls reduced the coefficients substantially (Table 4). This sex role dimension, however, was not related at all to additional intended children. Absolutely no relationship was found between current parity and *Opposed Special Privileges,* and this sex role dimension also had no effect on additional or total intended children. There was a positive net relationship between current parity and *Women Passive.* However, this result did not appear when additional fertility was the dependent variable.

In the bottom panel of Table 4, the results of adding the four sex role variables simultaneously to the two basic models are shown. In those analyses only *Women Passive* and *Home Orientation* had positive coefficients in the current parity equation. Thus, it appears that these two variables indeed do have a net relationship with current parity while the other sex role variables do not. However, when additional childbearing and the total number intended was examined, the results were quite different. There, the only consistent positive results were for *Home Orientation.* For both dependent variables, *Home Orientation* maintained its positive and moderately sized coefficient. It therefore appears that *Home Orientation* had a role in influencing fertility intentions net of all the other variables examined.

The introduction of all four ideology variables into the basic models resulted in coefficients that were virtually zero for both *Job Prerogatives for Men* and *Opposed Special Privileges.* With this approach there were no statistically significant coefficients for either variable in the Model 2 analysis. This result is, therefore, consistent with the notion that these two sex role dimensions have no relationships with fertility net of the background variables and the other two sex role variables. It may, therefore, be that there are no direct causal links between *Job Prerogatives for Men* and *Opposed Special Privileges* and childbearing. Rather, the results are consistent with the hypothesis that the zero order relationships observed (Table 3) were produced by *Home Orientation, Women Passive,* and the background variables influencing both *Job Prerogatives for Men* and *Opposed Special Privileges* as well as childbearing.

*Sex Roles and Labor Force Participation.* The second stage of the analysis extended the investigation to the relationships between sex role attitudes and labor force participation. The zero order correlations between the sex role variables and the three work variables are shown in Table 3. Focusing on the sex role attitude correlations, the coefficients were consistent with the hypotheses suggested. The most traditional women were the least likely to be working now or in the future and had the least commitment to work. All the correlations were negative, and, with two exceptions, were large enough to discount the possibility that they were produced by sampling variability.

It should be observed that *Work Commitment* was generally more closely related to the sex role measures than were the other work variables. This result was probably due to the fact that actual and planned labor force participation were influenced by the conditions and constraints in which the respondent found herself. Factors such as income, needs, and health, which are not ideological in nature, undoubtedly influence actual participation greatly, while having only a small influence on work commitment itself. Indeed, the correlations between husband's income and *Working Now* were stronger than those between income and *Work Commitment,* consistent with the interpretation that actual or expected work contains more reality constraints and less ideological influence than does work commitment.

Perhaps the most striking results were the substantial correlations between *Home Orientation* and the labor force variables (Table 3). *Home Orientation* had correlations with negative values greater than $r = -.2$ with the two actual work variables, while its correlation with *Work Commitment* ($r = -.3$) indicates a close relation between sex roles and this aspect of work. Additionally, the *Home Orientation* correlations were much larger than those for the other attitudinal variables.

The multivariate analysis proceeded in steps. First, age, religion, and race were controlled, a set of variables which are temporally and causally prior to either sex role attitudes or labor force orientation (Model 1). Model 2 controlled for all the variables just listed plus education, age at marriage and husband's income, which probably influence both attitudes and work and are also affected by them. Note, however, that in Model 2 the net relationship observed may not reflect the actual effect, since some of the total impact may operate indirectly through education, husband's income, and age at marriage.

The top panels of Table 5 show the results of adding the sex role variables one at a time to the basic models. In the bottom panels the four variables were added simultaneously. In all cases, only the coefficients for the sex role variables themselves are reported.

Looking at *Working Now* (upper panels of Table 5), the only variable with a consistent and substantial influence is *Home Orientation*. Its effect was important and only modestly decreased by the introduction of stronger controls in Model 2. However, the other sex role variables did not have significant coefficients when Model 2

ARLAND THORNTON AND DONALD CAMBURN

Table 5

Multivariate Anlaysis of the Relationship Between Current Labor
Force Participation, Current or Future Labor Force Participation, Work
Commitment, and Sex Role Attitudes[a]

| | Working Now | | Work Now or Future | | Work Commitment | |
|---|---|---|---|---|---|---|
| | Model 1 | Model 2 | Model 1 | Model 2 | Model 1 | Model 2 |
| **Variables Entered One at a Time** | | | | | | |
| Home orientation | -.26* | -.26* | -.28* | -.27* | -.30* | -.27* |
| Job prerogatives for men | -.02 | .00 | -.08* | -.06* | -.10* | -.06* |
| Opposed special privileges | -.02 | -.01 | -.08* | -.08* | .05* | -.06* |
| Women passive | -.03* | -.02 | .00 | .01 | -.04* | .00 |
| **Variables Entered Together** | | | | | | |
| Home orientation | -.28* | -.28* | -.28* | -.27* | -.29* | -.27* |
| Job Prerogatives for men | .05* | .05* | -.01 | .00 | -.03* | .00 |
| Opposed special privileges | .00 | .01 | -.04* | -.03* | .00 | -.01 |
| Women passive | .01 | .01 | .04* | .04* | .02 | .04* |

[a]Figures are standardized regression coefficients, N=5981.

Note: Besides the sex role variables the multivariate analysis for the three models
included the variables in the respective models in Table 4. The first set of coefficients
were obtained by separately including each sex role ideology in separate regression
equations. The second set of coefficients were obtained by entering the four variables
into the same regression equation.

*Coefficient is at least two times its standard error. This assumes simple random
sampling and does not include the design effects resulting from the use of a complex
sample design in the 1970 NFS.

controls were applied, suggesting that these variables did not have
relationships with current work net of the other variables in the
equations.

The expected negative relations between the sex role variables
and *Working Now or Future* were stronger than when *Working Now*
was the dependent variable (Table 5). For this variable, the coefficients for *Job Prerogatives for Men* and *Opposed Special Privileges*
retained their negative, statistically significant levels. Again, however,
the results did not support the hypothesis of a negative relationship
existing between *Women Passive* and work.

Also in Table 5, the relationship between the ideological variables and *Work Commitment* is shown, and again *Home Orientation* had a substantial negative coefficient which persisted in all
models while *Job Prerogatives for Men* and *Opposed Special
Privileges* maintained negative effects. And, as with the other dependent variables, there was no net influence of *Women Passive*.

Examination of all four of the sex role attitude variables together
was done by adding them simultaneously to the two basic models

that were used previously. The results of this approach (lower panels of Table 5) indicate that *Home Orientation* was clearly the dominant sex role variable. With the four variables examined together, *Home Orientation* was the only one retaining its negative coefficient while the coefficients of the other three sex role variables were substantially reduced. In fact, other than *Home Orientation*, all the Model 2 coefficients, except one, were either too small to be statistically significant or had positive signs. These results, therefore, are inconsistent with the hypothesis of there being a net negative relationship between the latter three sex role variables and the three measures of work. In addition, since *Home Orientation* is the only sex role variable that had a substantial relationship with the work variables, it is also the only one that could influence fertility *through* labor force participation. Any impact of the other three variables must operate through another mechanism.

*Sex Role Attitudes and Fertility Controlling Labor Force Participation.* Finally, to evaluate the extent to which there were relationships between the sex role attitudes and fertility net of the labor force variables, stage 3 of the analysis added two work variables (*Work Commitment* and either *Working Now* or *Work Now or Future*) to the fertility models. It should be noted that since these work variables are probably influenced by and influence childbearing, these controls were probably too strict, because effects as well as causes of fertility were controlled.

Earlier, it was noted that *Home Orientation* was positively related to current parity, even with controls for several other variables (Model 2 of Table 4). However, the introduction of the work variables into the analysis completely eliminated the relationship between *Home Orientation* and current parity. This observation, coupled with the substantial association between *Home Orientation* and the work variables suggests that the association between *Home Orientation* and current parity is moderated entirely by work experience and commitment. On the other hand, the moderate association between *Home Orientation* and additional intended children reported in Table 4 was not reduced with the introduction of controls for the labor force variables. Apparently, there is an association between this sex role variable and fertility intentions that does not operate through the work variables.

The association between *Women Passive* and current parity was not affected by controlling work experience and commitment. Without the work controls the coefficient for *Women Passive* was .04

ARLAND THORNTON AND DONALD CAMBURN

Table 6

Multivariate Analysis of the Relationship Between Current Parity,
Additional Intended Children, and Total Intended Children and Sex Role
Attitudes and Labor Force Participation: 1970 National Fertility Study[a]

| | Current Parity | Additional Intended Children | Total Intended Children |
|---|---|---|---|
| Variables Entered One at a Time | | | |
| Home orientation | -.01 | .07[*] | .06[*] |
| Job prerogatives for men | .02 | .01 | .02 |
| Opposed special privileges | -.01 | .01 | .00 |
| Women passive | .04[*] | -.02[*] | .03[*] |
| Variables Entered Together | | | |
| Home orientation | -.02 | .08[*] | .05[*] |
| Job prerogatives for men | .02 | .00 | .02 |
| Opposed special privileges | -.01 | .00 | -.01 |
| Women passive | .04[*] | -.03[*] | .02 |
| N=5981 | | | |

[a]Figures are standardized regression coefficients, N=5981.

Note: Besides the sex role variables, the multivariate analysis included all controls in Model 2 of Table 4. In addition to these controls, this analysis includes Work Commitment and Work Now or Future when additional or total intended children were the dependent variable and Working Now and Work Commitment when current parity was the dependent variable.

[*]Coefficient is at least two times its standard error. This assumes simple random sampling and does not include the design effects resulting from the use of a complex sample design in the 1970 NFS.

(Table 4) and there was no change with the introduction of the work variables (Table 6). These data, therefore, indicate that the causal mechanisms producing the association between these variables must operate independently of the work variables. This conclusion is further buttressed by the data in Table 5, which suggest that *Women Passive* does not have a substantial association with work variables.

## DISCUSSION

This research has investigated the interrelationships between several sex role attitudes, labor force participation, and childbearing. The analysis investigated the overall relationships among sex role attitudes, fertility, and labor force participation, as well as examining the extent to which the relationships between sex role attitudes and fertility worked through labor force participation and commitment. While four separate dimensions of sex role attitudes were investigated, the data indicate that only one, *Home Orientation,* was related to female employment, and that only *Home Orientation* and *Women Passive* were related to fertility.

The *Women Passive* variable displayed a moderate positive association with current parity and with total intended fertility, and was shown to operate independently of work experience and commitment. However, this sex role attitude variable displayed no positive association with the number of additional children intended. These observations are consistent with the notion that perceptions about inability to plan and perceptions about sex being primarily for men were related mostly to past childbearing rather than to future plans. It is thus possible that the positive coefficients for current parity were produced by planning failures. Either those who were negative about the ability of women to plan had more unplanned childbearing than others, or their unplanned fertility reduced their feelings of efficacy, as well as making them feel less positive about sex.

The role of unplanned fertility in the relationship between *Women Passive* and current parity was investigated by introducing the planning factor into the model explicitly. To accomplish this, a dummy variable was created which indicated whether or not any of the woman's children were unwanted (unwanted meant that prior to becoming pregnant, the woman would have preferred not to have had any more children). The results (not shown) indeed indicated the expected positive, but moderate, relationship between *Women Passive* and having unwanted children. In addition, the introduction of the unwanted fertility variable into the analysis reduced the size of the observed coefficients of *Women Passive* on current parity (again, results not shown). While the reduction was in the order of 50%, the coefficients were still positive and large enough to be statistically significant. So while unwanted fertility appears to have been part of the explanation of the observed relationship, apparently it could not account for the entire effect.

The *Home Orientation* variable was related to both fertility and labor force participation. The role of *Home Orientation* was particularly central in the analysis of labor force participation and commitment. While the zero order correlations for the other three sex role variables were negative as predicted, they were much weaker than those observed for *Home Orientation*. In addition, when all four sex role variables were examined together (bottom panel of Table 5), only *Home Orientation* had a significant negative relationship with the work variables. It is plausible to argue that orientation towards the home is a central element of sex roles and that it is a very important dimension in women's lives, since it determines how they spend their time and where their energy is most needed. Being such an important aspect, this orientation probably influences attitudes toward *Job Prerogatives for Men, Opposed Special Privileges,* and *Women Passive.* If this is true, it is also reasonable to argue that the observed correlations between the three latter variables and work were the result of these variables being related to *Home Orientation* rather than influencing or being influenced by the work variables.

The results reflect the central and vital role of *Home Orientation* in defining women's status and place. Women who scored high on this variable viewed women's place as being in the home and probably valued that status. In addition, they indicated that they saw a conflict between fulfilling that role and working; for them, work was seen as producing difficulty in carrying out domestic responsibilities. Therefore, it was not surprising that these women were less committed to work. Apparently, they were less likely to see work as a way to obtain fulfillment, did not feel the need to have a career, and were much less likely to be working at the time of the interview.

The relationship between *Home Orientation* and female employment also had implications for understanding the relationship between *Home Orientation* and fertility. It is likely that part of the positive association between fertility and this sex role attitude was produced by *Home Orientation* decreasing labor force participation and commitment, which in turn increased fertility. This causal interpretation is supported by the fact that when labor force activity was included in the analysis of current parity, the *Home Orientation* coefficient was reduced to zero (Table 6). On the other hand, the analysis of additional and total intended children indicates that *Home Orientation* had an influence on fertility which was not mediated through labor force activity. In those analyses, the moderate positive coefficient for *Home Orientation* was maintained despite the introduction of the labor force variable. These results, therefore, suggest that there are both direct and indirect mechanisms transmitting the influence of home orientation to childbearing.

This research indicates a modest association between two dimensions of sex role attitudes and childbearing. Furthermore, the results indicate that, to some extent, sex role attitudes operate through work to influence fertility. While the results of this research depend upon cross-sectional data, it is likely that the changes occurring in American attitudes toward sex roles are related to the trends also occurring in the fertility and labor force participation of women; trends in one of these areas probably have consequences for the other two. Therefore, it is important that additional research be conducted to identify the precise nature of the causal forces operating so that the direct, indirect, and reciprocal mechanisms producing the pattern of observed correlations can be isolated and estimated.

## REFERENCES

Bumpass, L. R. Fertility differences by employment patterns and role attitudes (Working Paper 74-23). Center for Demography and Ecology, The University of Wisconsin, 1974.

Clarkson, F. E., Vogel, S. R., Broverman, I. K., & Broverman, D. M. Family size and sex role stereotypes. *Science*, 1970, 390–392.

Goldberg, D. Modernism: The extensiveness of women's roles and attitudes. *World Fertility Survey Occasional Paper No. 14*. International Statistical Institute, 1974.

Goldberg, D. Socioeconomic theory and differential fertility: The case of the LDC's. *Social Forces*, 1975, *54* (September).

Hoffman, L. W., & Wyatt, F. Social change and motivations for having larger families: Some theoretical considerations. *Merrill-Palmer Quarterly*, 1960.

Mason, K., & Bumpass, L. U.S. women's sex-role ideology, 1970. *American Journal of Sociology*, 1975, *80*, 1212–1219.

Mason, K., Czajka, J., & Arber, S. Change in U.S. women's sex-role attitudes, 1964–1974. *American Sociological Review*, 1976, *41*, 513–596.

Oppenheimer, V. K. The sociology of women's economic role in the family. *American Sociological Review*, 1977, *42*, 387–406.

Rainwater, L. *Family design: Marital sexuality, family size and contraception*. Chicago: Aldine, 1965.

Scanzoni, J. *Sex roles, life styles, and childbearing*. New York: The Free Press, 1975.

Waite, L. J., & Stolzenberg, R. M. Intended childbearing and labor force participation of young women: Insights from nonrecursive models. *American Sociological Review*, 1976, *41*, 235–252.

Westoff, C. F., & Ryder, N. B. The contraceptive revolution. Princeton: Princeton University Press, 1977.

# Timing of the Decision To Remain Voluntarily Childless:
# Evidence for Continuous Socialization

Sharon K. Houseknecht

*Ohio State University*

This study contrasts different types of voluntary childlessness. Women who decided to remain childless relatively early in life, before marriage (*early articulators*) were compared with women who did not decide until after they had married and developed a preferred life style that did not include children (*postponers*). The comparison centered on a previously formulated model that explained the decision to remain childless in terms of family background factors, autonomy and achievement orientation in adulthood, and reference group support. The major difference disclosed by this research was with respect to family background factors. In addition to the early versus later decision to remain childless, socialization patterns in the family of orientation differentiate the two types of voluntarily childless women.

Some earlier research by this author (1974, 1977a, 1978) produced findings that suggested the basis for a social psychological model of voluntary childlessness. This model explains the decision to remain childless in terms of: (a) family background factors; (b) self-other attitudes; and (c) reference groups. Certain family background factors are seen as instigative in the development of autonomy and achievement orientation. These two characteristics, when accompanied by a preference for a childless life style, increase the likeli-

---

Thanks are due to Dr. Graham B. Spanier and Dr. Carolyn W. Sherif for their thoughtful guidance at all stages of the research. Sincere appreciation is also extended to Roger T. Richards for his constructive advice in preparing this manuscript.

82

PSYCHOLOGY OF WOMEN QUARTERLY

hood that a women will choose that life style, particularly when these various attitudes are sustained through reference group support.

In the first exploratory study of voluntarily childless wives, Veevers (1973) suggested that there are two different types of people who remain voluntarily childless. One type expresses intentions to remain childless relatively early in life, even prior to marriage. The other type arrives at a childless decision through a series of postponements after marriage. These two types have been referred to as *early articulators* and *postponers,* respectively (Houseknecht, 1974; 1977a). The selection procedure that was followed in the present study produced a childless sample composed of a mixture of married early articulators and married postponers. Although these women could not specify the exact point in time that they had decided to remain permanently childless, they had no difficulty in reporting whether or not the decision was made before marriage and before meeting their husbands.

A major objective in this research was to compare these two types of voluntarily childless women with regard to the previously-formulated model. It is suggested that there are at least two different paths to choosing a childless life style. Are there factors that distinguish women who opt for voluntary childlessness early in life from women who do so some time after they are married?

## METHODS

### Sample

Personal, in-depth interviews were conducted with 51 currently married women who reported themselves to be childless by choice. The women were located by means of a modified network approach. An initial list of names suggested by family planning clinics, hospitals, the National Organization for Nonparents (NON), and various other persons in administrative positions was compiled. This procedure was used to guard against the possible bias of the reference group data that might have occurred if respondents had been asked to recommend other potential respondents.

Six criteria determined whether a childless woman was accepted for participation in the study. In addition to affirming that she had never borne a child nor adopted one, she also had to state clearly that her childlessness was due to choice, not biological reasons. She also had to have been married for a minimum of five years if neither she nor her spouse had been voluntarily sterilized for contraceptive purposes. (Only 8% of the respondents, all *early articulators,* had not been married for five years.) An additional measure of commitment was an attitude certainty measure. Each woman had to answer, "very certain" or "fairly certain" that no children were desired in the future. Finally, all of the respondents had to be between 25 and 40 years of age.

Although the research design did not require or even suggest it, the proportions of *early articulators* and *postponers* that participated in this study closely approximated the distribution that was found by earlier investigators (Bram, 1974; Veevers, 1973). Postponement seems to be the more common route to childlessness with about two-thirds of the women falling into this category. Only about one-third of the women identified themselves as *early articulators*. The final sample consisted of 32 *postponers* and 19 *early articulators*. Selected social characteristics of the sample are summarized in Table 1. A more detailed account is provided in Houseknecht (1977b).

## Operationalization of Concepts

*Family Background Factors.*   One study that examined family background factors in connection with the decision to have or not to have chil-

Table 1

Selected Social Characteristics by Type of Childlessness

| Characteristic | Early Articulators | Postponers |
|---|---|---|
| Mean age | 30.3 | 29.7 |
| Mean years married | 6.6 | 7.8 |
| Per cent in labor force | 95 | 97 |
| Education: | | |
| Per cent high school | 5 | 9 |
| Per cent 1-3 years beyond high school | 16 | 16 |
| Per cent 4 years beyond high school | 26 | 25 |
| Per cent 5-6 years beyond high school | 42 | 50 |
| Per cent 7 or more years beyond high school | 11 | 0 |
| Religion: | | |
| Per cent atheist, agnostic, none | 58 | 50 |
| Per cent Catholic | 0 | 13 |
| Per cent Jewish | 5 | 0 |
| Per cent Protestant | 37 | 37 |
| | (N = 19) | (N = 32) |

dren concluded that there is a weak association between family history and the decision to remain childless (Bram, 1974). Another study (Ory, 1976), looking primarily at demographic variables, found no relationship between voluntary childlessness and family of orientation characteristics for females. Investigating the contribution of childhood family variables to sex-role ideology, Lipman-Blumen (1972) also found no demographic distinctions. She was alert, however, to the possible existence of more subtle factors. One distinguishing influence that she discovered was the "development of a psychological distance from parents during adolescence." Women with a contemporary ideology were more likely than those with the traditional ideology to evolve a sense of separateness as individuals during adolescence.

Anticipating that the contemporary ideology might relate to a decision to remain childless, a previous study by this author (Houseknecht, 1974; 1978) explored this same factor to see if it differentiated *early articulators* from females who desired children. The data revealed *early articulators* were significantly more likely to develop a psychological distance from parents during adolescence. To learn if *early articulators* differed from *post-poners* in this respect, psychological distance was operationally defined in the present study as the extent to which the respondents believed that they had developed attitudes in adolescence that differed from their parents.

Retrospective reports on other family background factors were also obtained. Moderate levels of family warmth, a relatively permissive rather than coercive pattern of parental authority, independence training, and encouragement of achievement have been found to be associated with adult autonomy and achievement orientation for females. The implication of this socialization data, according to Stein and Bailey (1973), is that childrearing practices that are conducive to feminine sex typing are often antagonistic to those that lead to achievement-oriented behavior and autonomy. Achievement-oriented behavior and emotional independence are traditionally unfeminine characteristics.

A family warmth index (Rapoport & Rapoport, 1971) was constructed by scoring the respondent's characterization of each family relationship on a scale from "extremely close" to "not close at all" and averaging the scores.

.  Coerciveness was measured by administering four subscales of the first version of the Cornell Parent Behavior Description Instrument (Bronfenbrenner, 1961). The subscales used assessed physical discipline (corporal punishment), affective discipline (guilt incitement), indulgent discipline (excessive leniency), and principled discipline (democratic order).

Scale items for examining parental expectations for assertive autonomy were derived from the cluster of items representing "Encouragement of Independence and Individuality" in Baumrind's Parent Behavior Ratings (1971). Parental encouragement for achievement efforts was tested with the "achievement demands" subscale of the Cornell Parent Behavior Description Instrument (Bronfenbrenner, 1961).

Respondents were asked to rate both parents separately on all of the above scales.

SHARON K. HOUSEKNECHT

## Self-Other Attitudes

*Autonomy.* It was reasoned that although the childless women would not be without some reinforcement for their decision, they would be sufficiently autonomous to remain unaffected by countervailing pressures and sanctions exerted by other reference groups and the dominant society. Degree of autonomy was assessed by (a) an autonomy scale that measured self-determination; (b) the mean number of reference groups indicated by the two types of childless women; and (c) a measure of concern for negative pressures and sanctions that accompany the childless state.

An appropriate autonomy scale to measure self-determination was unavailable. Therefore, a Likert-type scale was developed based on reference group theory. The reliability coefficient using Cronbach's coefficient alpha was .80.

Cantril's (1963) "self-anchoring" scale was used to measure degree of concern for pressures and sanctions. Each respondent was shown a drawing of a ladder with 10 rungs. The interviewer asked each woman to indicate the place on the ladder that corresponded to how much she was concerned when she experienced pressures and sanctions from various sources such as parents, in-laws, friends, relatives.

*Achievement.* In the present study, achievement orientation was operationalized as factors predisposing a woman to strive for success outside the home. Such factors included (a) acceptance of roles other than wife-mother; (b) commitment to such roles; (c) life goals that attribute import to success in a vocational role; and (d) a tendency to place a greater value on own achievements than the achievements of others. One consequence of a predisposition to strive for success outside the home may be that childbearing is viewed as only one of several sources of fulfillment and, therefore, becomes more of a choice.

*Acceptance of Roles Other Than Wife-Mother.* The subscale of the Attitudes Toward Women Scale (Spence & Helmreich, 1972) dealing with vocational, educational, and intellectual roles for women was used to measure acceptance of roles other than those of wife-mother.

*Life Goals.* To see whether both types of childless women considered success in a vocational role as an important life goal, they were asked, "What best describes the kind of accomplishment which for you would represent achievement or success?"

*Occupational Commitment.* To test the two samples for a difference in work commitment (degree of ego involvement that a woman has in her work), a number of questions were posed. The first question asked about the woman's present role and then about her role preference to see if there was a discrepancy. A hypothetical situation was presented to see if the woman would move for the sake of her own career advancement even if her husband did not want to move and leave his job. To further test for employment commitment, each woman was asked her major reason for working outside the home. Finally, work commitment was measured by the "method of ordered alternatives" development by Sherif and Sherif (1969), a type of attitude scale construction that allows indirect attitude measurement and assessment of degree of ego involvement.

*Mode of Achievement.* Studies have shown that women tend to derive their status from the males to whom they are attached (Felson & Knoke, 1974; Lipman-Blumen, 1972). To measure mode of achievement, each woman was asked, "Would you say that you experience the greatest sense of satisfaction from your own accomplishments, your husband's accomplishments, or both equally?"

## Reference Groups

To measure conformity to normative referents with respect to the childbearing decision, a version of the multiple-item instrument developed by Ewens and Ehrlich (1972) was used. Four different measures of reference group support were included. First, however, it was necessary to compile an all-inclusive list of reference groups. Twelve different items asked respondents to name the people and groups in their home towns and elsewhere who had become very important to them since their marriage.*

Two measures of reference group support for childlessness were concerned with the *existence* and the *extent* of support. In this connection, the respondents were asked to indicate whether each person or group on the list would approve, be indifferent toward, or disapprove of their decision not to have children. Reflecting perceived attitudes, this information permitted each respondent's attitude toward childlessness to be compared with that of their reference groups whom they reported as having been influential in their childbearing decision. The analysis disclosed (a) the existence of *any* support at all for the choice to remain childless and (b) the extent of that support as revealed in the proportion of reference groups who approved.

A third measure of normative referents for the childbearing decision was the acceptable family size range for each reference group on the list as perceived by the respondents. The respondents were asked how many children they thought each person or group on their list would say would make a family "too small" and how many would make it "too large."

A final measure of reference group support for childlessness was concerned with the importance ascribed by the respondents to those reference groups whom they perceived as approving of childlessness and to those whom they perceived as disapproving. The intent here was to see if the *early articulators* differed from the *postponers* in the extent to which they considered reference groups who *approved* of childlessness to be "very important."

---

* The author has corrected this statement to read, " Twelve different items asked respondents to name the people and groups in their hometowns and elsewhere who had been most important to them before their marriage, as well as those who had become very important to them since their marriage." --Ed.

SHARON K. HOUSEKNECHT

Reference group support for each respondent's decision was ultimately determined by asking each woman *whose opinions* (among those people and groups that she had listed as being most important in her life) she had considered in her decision not to have children. The analyses for the above measures were based on this select group, not all of the reference groups that had been mentioned. In general, the influence of a particular reference group is not totally pervasive. People have different reference groups in different spheres of life. Consequently, in this study it was necessary to investigate separately those people whose opinions were considered important with regard to childbearing. Nevertheless, all reference groups had to be ascertained initially to help reduce selective recall.

## RESULTS

The results reveal a number of similarities between the *early articulators* and the *postponers* (Table 2). Major distinctions that were

Table 2

A Comparison of Two Types of Voluntary Childless Women: Summary of Findings and Statistical Tests

| Variable | Early Articulators | Postponers | $\chi^2$ | t-test | df | p |
|---|---|---|---|---|---|---|
| Autonomy | | | | | | |
| A. Self-determination--mean scale score | 55.79 (19) | 61.03 (32) | | 1.85 | 49 | N.S. |
| B. Mean number of reference groups whose opinions were considered in the childbearing decision | 4.32 (19) | 5.50 (32) | | .84 | 49 | N.S. |
| C. Sanction concern--mean scale score | 32.10 (19) | 27.09 (32) | | 1.04 | 49 | N.S. |
| Achievement Orientation | | | | | | |
| A. Awareness and acceptance of alternative roles--mean scale score | 48.57 (19) | 47.62 (32) | | 1.16 | 49 | N.S. |
| B. Life goals that emphasize success in vocational roles | 74% (19) | 66% (32) | .80 | | 2 | N.S. |
| C. Occupational commitment | | | | | | |
| 1. Willingness to move for own career advancement | 79% (19) | 69% (32) | .21 | | 1 | N.S. |
| 2. Nonfinancial motive for employment exclusively | 67% (18) | 55% (31) | .26 | | 1 | N.S. |
| 3. Occupational ego-involvement-- | | | | | | |
| accepted statements ($\bar{X}$) | 2.8 (18) | 2.9 (31) | | .42 | 47 | N.S. |
| rejected statements ($\bar{X}$) | 2.8 (18) | 3.1 (31) | | .97 | 47 | N.S. |
| D. Vicarious mode of achievement | 0 (19) | 0 (32) | .01 | | 1 | N.S. |

PSYCHOLOGY OF WOMEN QUARTERLY

Table 3

Perception of Psychological Distance from Family

During Adolescence by Type of Childlessness

| Psychological Distance | Early Articulators | Postponers |
|---|---|---|
| Own attitudes and parents' attitudes very different | 48% | 31% |
| Own attitudes and parents' attitudes slightly different | 47 | 31 |
| Own attitudes and parents' attitudes not different at all | 5 | 38 |
| | 100% | 100% |
| | (N = 19) | (N = 32) |

$\chi^2 = 6.52$

df = 2

p < .04

found involved family background factors and the extent of reference group support (Tables 3 to 8).

## Family Background Factors

*Psychological Distance From Parents During Adolescence.* The *early articulators* were significantly more likely than the postponers to report the development of a psychological distance between self and parents during adolescence. Recall that psychological distance was operationally defined in this study as "differing attitudes." As Table 3 shows, only 5% of the *early articulators* in contrast to 38% of the *postponers* said that their attitudes and their parents' attitudes had not differed at all during adolescence, $\chi(2) = 6.52$, <.04.

*Level of Warmth in the Family of Orientation.* A second background factor that distinguished the two types of childless women was level of warmth in the family of orientation. The findings presented in Table 4 suggest a moderate level of overall family warmth

Table 4

Scores on Family Warmth in Family of Orientation[a] by Type of Childlessness

| | Early Articulators | | | | Postponers | | | |
| Family Warmth | Mean | Standard Deviation | Standard Error | | Mean | Standard Deviation | Standard Error | t-test |
|---|---|---|---|---|---|---|---|---|
| Family Warmth – Total | 2.69 | .546 | .125 | | 3.05 | .548 | .097 | 2.25* |
| Family Warmth – Parents only | 2.68 | .711 | .163 | | 3.10 | .780 | .138 | 1.94 |
| Family Warmth – Mother only | 2.89 | .875 | .201 | | 3.31 | .821 | .145 | 1.71 |
| Family Warmth – Father only | 2.47 | 1.020 | .234 | | 2.90 | .893 | .158 | 1.59 |
| | | (N = 19) | | | | (N = 32) | | |

[a]The range of possible scores is 1 to 4:  1 = Not close at all

2 = Slightly close

3 = Fairly close

4 = Extremely close

*p < .03

Table 5

Scores[a] on Achievement Demands in Family of Orientation[b] by Type of Childlessness

| | Early Articulators | | | | Postponers | | | |
| Achievement Demands | Mean | Standard Deviation | Standard Error | | Mean | Standard Deviation | Standard Error | t-test |
|---|---|---|---|---|---|---|---|---|
| Achievement Demands – Total | 2.98 | .966 | .222 | | 2.32 | .833 | .147 | 2.57* |
| Achievement Demands – Mother only | 3.20 | .984 | .226 | | 2.35 | .806 | .142 | 2.22** |
| Achievement Demands – Father only | 2.76 | 1.044 | .240 | | 2.30 | .952 | .168 | 1.64 |
| | | (N = 19) | | | | (N = 32) | | |

[a]Based on the "achievement demands" subscale of the Cornell Parent Behavior Description Instrument (Bronfenbrenner, 1961).

[b]The range of possible scores is 1 to 5.

*p < .02

**p < .01

Table 6

Scores[a] on Various Types of Parental Discipline in Family of Orientation[b] by Type of Childlessness

| Types of Parental Discipline | Early Articulators | | | Postponers | | |
|---|---|---|---|---|---|---|
| | Mean | Standard Deviation | Standard Error | Mean | Standard Deviation | Standard Error |
| Physical Discipline | 1.90 | .566 | .130 | 1.62 | .488 | .086 |
| Affective Discipline | 2.11 | .639 | .147 | 1.89 | .650 | .115 |
| Indulgent Discipline | 2.32 | .546 | .125 | 2.23 | .728 | .129 |
| Principled Discipline | 3.38 | .635 | .146 | 3.92 | .797 | .141 |
| | | (N = 19) | | | (N = 32) | |

[a]Based on the Physical Discipline, Affective Discipline, Indulgent Discipline, and Principled Discipline Subscales of the Cornell Parent Behavior Description Instrument (Bronfenbrenner, 1961).

[b]The range for each type of discipline score is 1 to 5 with the higher number indicating a greater frequency of occurrence.

$F(3,147) = 3.72$

$p < .05$

t test of physical discipline = N.S.

t test on affective discipline = N.S.

t test on indulgent discipline = N.S.

t test of principled discipline = 2.52, 49 df, $p < .02$

Table 7

Scores[a] on Assertive Autonomy in Family of Orientation[b] by Type of Childlessness

| Assertive Autonomy | Early Articulators | | | Postponers | | | t-test |
|---|---|---|---|---|---|---|---|
| | Mean | Standard Deviation | Standard Error | Mean | Standard Deviation | Standard Error | |
| Assertive Autonomy - Total | 2.75 | .533 | .122 | 3.28 | .813 | .144 | 2.55** |
| Assertive Autonomy - Mother only | 2.92 | .725 | .166 | 3.47 | .827 | .146 | 2.40** |
| Assertive Autonomy - Father only | 2.57 | .742 | .170 | 3.08 | .910 | .161 | 2.06* |
| | | (N = 19) | | | (N = 19) | | |

[a]Based on the cluster of items representing "Encouragement of Independence and Individuality" in Baumrind's Parent Behavior Ratings (1971).

[b]The range of possible scores is 1 to 5.

*$p < .05$

**$p < .02$

Table 8

Mean Distribution of Reference Group Support for Childless Decision[a] by Type of Childlessness

|  | Only Reference Groups Whose Opinions Were Considered in Childbearing Decision | | |
|  | Early Articulators | Postponers | $t_7$-test |
|---|---|---|---|
| Approved of Childlessness | .62 | .79 | 1.95* |
| Disapproved of Childlessness | .16 | .14 | .41 |
| Approved - Considered Very Important | .77 | .86 | 1.01 |
| Disapproved - Considered Very Important | .32 | .30 | .18 |
| Proportion of Reference-Others Whose Lower Limit of Acceptable Family Size is Childlessness | .60 | .73 | 1.29 |
| Proportion of Reference-Others Whose Upper Limit of Acceptable Family Size is Greater Than Three Children | .25 | .25 | .02 |

[a]Proportions were used as indicators of reference group support because of the wide range in the number of important people and groups designated by each respondent and, therefore, were treated as scores.

*p < .05

for both types of childless women. However, *early articulators* do report experiencing a significantly lower level of warmth in their family of orientation, $\overline{X} = 2.69$, than do the *postponers*, $\overline{X} = 3.05$; t (49) = 2.25, p<.03.

*Achievement Demands.* A third significant family background variable was demand for achievement. Table 5 shows that the parents of the *early articulators* were seen as more likely to stress achievement efforts, $\overline{X} = 2.98$, than the parents of the *postponers*, $\overline{X} = 2.32$; t (49) = 2.57 p<.02. However, it is apparent that achievement encouragement from the mother was mainly responsible for this observed difference, $\overline{X} = 3.20$ and 2.35, respectively; t (49) = 3.33, p<.01.

*Parental Authority Pattern.* A fourth family background factor that differentitated the two types of childless women was degree of perceived coercive parental authority. Recall that the four subscales that were used to determine degree of coerciveness were physical discipline, affective discipline, indulgent discipline, and principled discipline. Since each respondent had a score for each type of discipline, analysis of variance for repeated measures was used in computing the extent of the difference within and between the two samples. The results indicate that there was an interaction between the various types of discipline and types of childlessness, $F$ (3, 147) = 3.72, $p<.05$. In other words, the discipline pattern for the *early articulators* differed from that for the *postponers*. As shown in Table 6, both samples of women scored highest on principled discipline (the mean for the *early articulators* was 3.38 and for the *postponers* it was 3.92). Postponers scored significantly higher, however, $t$ (49) = 2.52, $p<.02$.

*Assertive Autonomy.* The results presented in Table 7 reveal a fifth family background factor differentiating the two types of childless women. The parents of the *postponers* were significantly more likely to be perceived as encouraging assertive autonomy, $\overline{X} = 3.28$, than the parents of the *early articulators*, $\overline{X}$ = 2.75; $t$ (49) = 2.55, $p<.02$. These differences held for both the mothers and the fathers when the two were considered separately.

## Reference Groups

*Extent of Reference Group Support.* Turning now to reference group support for the childless decision (Table 8), the findings reveal that the average proportion of reference groups whose opinions were considered in the childbearing decision and who approved of childlessness was somewhat higher for the *postponers*, .79, than for the *early articulators*, .62; $t$ (49) = 1.95, $p<.05$. However, none of the other measures of reference group support revealed any notable differences.

## Voluntary Sterilization and Divorce

Two unexpected findings merit mention. One pertains to the degree of commitment to the childless decision exhibited by the two types of women in the sample. Voluntary sterilization for contraceptive purposes represents an incontestable behavioral measure of commitment to childlessness beyond the previously discussed commitment criteria that were used for respondent selection.

Comparing the *early articulators* and the *postponers*, the findings show that voluntary sterilization of either the wife and/or husband characterized 74% of the *early articulators* in contrast to only 31% of the *postponers*. In only two instances were both the husband and wife sterilized, and both of these cases involved *early articulators*. Assuming that voluntary sterilization represents an extreme measure of commitment to the childless decision, the results suggest that, in general, the *early articulators* exhibited a greater degree of commitment than did the *postponers*.

A second unexpected finding revealed that a significantly greater number of *early articulators* than *postponers* had previously been divorced, 31.6% versus 3.1%, respectively; $t(49) = 5.92$, $p<.02$. It could be that the efforts of the *early articulators* to persuade their spouses to accept a childless life style are less effective and more stressful than in the case of the *postponers* where the decision evolves after marriage out of the couple relationship.

## DISCUSSION

The fact that most of the women in this study did not decide to remain childless until after they were married and had participated in alternative roles outside the home reflects continuous socialization with regard to fertility decisions over the life span. Further support for continuous socialization was provided when the *postponers* were compared with the *early articulators*. Recall that the major distinctions found between these two samples involved family background factors and extent of reference group support.

The *early articulators* reported being exposed to more extensive parental demands for achievement efforts than did the *postponers*. Perhaps as a result of being pushed to achieve, the *early articulators* were not so concerned with the issue of motherhood. Their most immediate concern conceivably could have been those activities in which they could demonstrate successful achievement efforts, since that was a value highly emphasized in their families. Furthermore, they may have been less inclined to replicate a family life where there was significantly less warmth and attitude compatibility than that depicted by the *postponers* for their family of orientation.

In contrast, the *postponers'* parents were reported to have provided more encouragement for assertive autonomy than parents of the *early articulators*. This finding is consistent with the *postponers'* higher score on principled (democratic) discipline. The *postponers* perhaps had no reason to opt against having children prior to adulthood given their greater family warmth and attitude compatibility.

However, once they did have a reason, such as achievement activities outside the home, they may have been predisposed to decide in terms of what they considered their best interests, since they had been strongly encouraged throughout their childhood to make their own decisions and consider their own opinions.

It must be stressed that regardless of the stage in the life cycle in which the decision to remain childless is made, it is generally not made without reference group support. The results of earlier research demonstrated the importance of reference group support for a sample of unmarried *early articulators* (Houseknecht, 1974; 1977a). The findings in the present study substantiate that this was also the case for both the married *early articulators* and the married *postponers,* even though the *postponers* had more extensive reference group support for their childless decision than did the *early articulators.*

In summary, there is no single temporal pattern for choosing the childless option. Assuming that social approval for childlessness is available, the development of an achievement orientation which might increase awareness of the advantages of a childless life style may not occur until after the woman has married and become involved in alternative roles outside the home. Decisions not to have children, then, are made at various stages of the life cycle by different women. The findings in this study suggest that family background factors, in addition to social approval, may enable the *early articulators* to elect childlessness as a preferred life style at a relatively early age. Other women are exposed to influences at a later point in their lives which can have the same effect.

It is important to note as a final addendum that there are some reasons why the findings reported in this study must be interpreted with caution. First, since the mean years of age and the mean age at marriage did not differ significantly between the *early articulators* and the *postponers,* it is clear that they made their decision to remain childless in different historical periods, not just different life cycle periods. One way to reduce this source of bias would be to compare *early articulators* and *postponers,* all of whom made their decision at the same point in historical time. Unfortunately, this approach would mean that the *early articulators* and the *postponers* belonged to different cohorts and this difference would be open to even more serious criticism. Also, it has already been noted that most women cannot specify the *exact* point in time that they decided to remain childless even though they have no difficulty in reporting whether or not the decision was made before or after marriage.

A second limitation of this study is its reliance on retrospective reports. Although retrospective reports are acknowledged to be problematic, they are still commonly employed when they provide the only viable means for studying certain variables. In the case of the present topic, a very small proportion of women remain permanently childless, which renders impractical any type of longitudinal design. Furthermore, childless intentions are not something that can be selected for in childhood, as illustrated in the case of the *postponers.*

## CONCLUSIONS

With the exception of one study that looked at *early articulators* exclusively (Houseknecht, 1974, 1977a, 1978), different types of voluntary childlessness have yet to be extensively researched. Exploration of distinctions is an important step in the process of building a substantive theory that will explain this complex phenomenon.

The present study compared women who had decided to remain childless relatively early in life with women who did not decide until after they were married. The results suggest that timing is not the only factor that differentiates these women. Timing appears to reflect different socialization patterns. These findings are relevant for policy makers because they demonstrate that, even with regard to choosing a childless life style, there is continuous socialization over the life cycle and, therefore, more than one possible point for intervention and attitude change.

Despite the different socialization patterns, however, the findings reveal that, in the case of both the *early articulators* and the *postponers,* the childrearing practices were conducive to the learning of "nontraditional" sex roles. Autonomy and achievement orientation in adulthood characterized both types of childless women. It is reasonable to assume that these two stereotypically non-feminine traits contribute to a greater latitude of freedom to choose a lifestyle that is compatible with personal needs and desires.

## REFERENCES

Baumrind, D. Current patterns of parental authority. *Developmental Psychology Monograph,* 1971, *4,* part 2.

Bram, S. *To have or have not: A social psychological study of voluntarily childless couples, parents-to-be, and parents.* Unpublished doctoral dissertation, University of Michigan, Ann Arbor, 1974.

Bronfenbrenner, U. Some familial antecedents of responsibility and leadership in adolescence. In L. Petrullo & B. L. Base (Eds.), *Leadership and Interpersonal Behavior.* New York: Holt, Rinehart, and Winston, 1961.

Cantril, H. A study of aspirations. *Scientific American,* 1963, *208,* 41–45.

Ewens, W. L., & Ehrlich, H. J. Reference-other support and ethnic attitudes as predictors of intergroup behavior. *The Sociological Quarterly,* 1972, *13,* 348–360.

Felson, M., & Knoke, D. Social status and the married woman. *Journal of Marriage and the Family,* 1974, *36,* 516–521.

Houseknecht, S. K. Reference group support for voluntary childlessness: Evidence for conformity. *Journal of Marriage and the Family,* 1977, *39,* 285–292. (a)

Houseknecht, S. K. *Social psychological aspects of voluntary childlessness.* Unpublished master's thesis, Pennsylvania State University, University Park, 1974.

Houseknecht, S. K. A social psychological model of voluntary childlessness. *Alternative Lifestyles: Changing Patterns in Marrige, Family and Intimacy,* 1978, *1,* in press.

Houseknecht, S. K. *Wives but not mothers: Factors influencing the decision to remain voluntarily childless.* Unpublished doctoral dissertation, Pennsylvania State University, University Park, 1977. (b)

Lipman-Blumen, J. How ideology shapes women's lives. *Scientific American,* 1972, *226,* 34–42.

Ory, M. *The decision to parent or not: Normative and structural components.* Unpublished doctoral dissertation, Purdue University, Lafayette, Indiana, 1976.

Rapoport, R., & Rapoport, R. N. Early and later experiences as determinants of adult behavior: Married women's family and career patterns. *British Journal of Sociology,* 1971, *22,* 16–30.

Sherif, M., & Sherif, C. W. *Social Psychology.* New York: Harper and Row Publishers, 1969.

Spence, J. T., & Helmreich, R. The attitudes toward women scale: An objective instrument to measure attitudes toward the rights and roles of women in contemporary society. JSAS *Catalog of Documents in Psychology,* 1972.

Stein, A. H., & Bailey, M. M. The socialization of achievement orientation in females. *Psychological Bulletin,* 1973, *80,* 345–366.

Veevers, J. E. Voluntarily childless wives: An exploratory study. *Sociology and Social Research,* 1973, *57,* 356–366.

# Roles and Role Conflict of Women in Infertile Couples

Janet R. Allison

*Western Montana Regional Community Mental Health Center*

This study explored the experience of role conflict for women in infertile couples. The infertile group consisted of 29 women who, with their husbands, were beginning an infertility program; comparison group subjects were 29 married women with no history of inability to conceive. Each subject completed self-report instruments measuring role conceptions and expectations, the experience of role conflict, and occupational commitment. Each husband also reported his role expectations for his ideal woman. Also, a semi-structured interview was conducted with each infertile subject. Compared to the control group, the infertile group's role conceptions were more traditional; they reported less role conflict of various kinds, and they showed greater occupational commitment. They did not differ significantly on degree of wife-husband role discrepancy, or on mother's occupational commitment. These findings lead to an understanding of infertility as part of an interactional system for dealing with potentially intolerable sources of role conflict.

Pregnancy is probably the most dramatic, strictly female biological event—one that has meaning not only biologically, but culturally, interpersonally, and intrapsychically as well. Fertility is closely tied to woman's identity and roles (Russo, 1976), and a psychology of women that is founded in women's own experience and values must address this area.

---

This article is based upon the author's doctoral dissertation, *Infertility and Role Conflict: A Phenomenological Study of Women.* Unpublished doctoral dissertation, California School of Professional Psychology, 1976. Requests for reprints should be sent to: Janet R. Allison, Western Montana Regional Community Mental Health Center, Building T-9, Fort Missoula Road, Missoula, Montana 59801.

Infertility has become a particularly interesting problem in the current ecological and social contexts. There is real world-wide necessity to control and reduce fertility. With the aid of the women's movement, extrafamilial roles for women that offer rewards and status competing with those offered by motherhood are becoming increasingly legitimized. Despite these changes, the woman who fails to become pregnant still tends to see herself, and often is seen by others, as somehow unnatural, shameful, a failure as a woman. Substantial medical resources each year are devoted to research to alleviate infertility. Recent advances in reproductive medicine that make fertilization possible outside the body reflect the view that infertility is a "problem" requiring priority attention by society.

## Psychological Aspects of Infertility

Literature on the motivation for and meaning of motherhood ranges from the thinking of some Freudians who assume motivation for motherhood to be natural, inevitable, and biologically-based (Benedek & Rubenstein, 1939; Deutsch, 1944; Freud, 1959a, 1959b) to that of some feminists who see motherhood as a cultural role trap for women (Jones, 1970; Mitchell, 1973). With the development of the women's movement and some new views on the psychology of women, some writers describe pregnancy as an almost inevitably ambivalent and ambiguous matter, given our present cultural context and role expectations (Bardwick, 1970; Bardwick & Douvan, 1971; Lott, 1973). Motivation for childbearing is a complex phenomenon, which involves biologically-based factors and social roles and expectations, including some response to the perceived demands and consequences involved in having children within the woman's specific situation (Clifford, 1962; Greenberg, Loesch, & Lakin, 1959; Hatcher, 1973).

Much of the literature that speculates about the relationship of psychological factors to infertility has arisen out of a psychoanalytic framework (Noyes & Chapnick, 1964). Its focus has been on "psychogenic" infertility in women, that is, infertility presumed to be caused by psychological factors since no organic dysfunction can be found (Benedek, 1970; Deutsch, 1945; Ford, Forman, Wilson, Char, Mixson, & Scholz, 1953; Mandy & Mandy, 1958). Most of this work, which has supported the notion that infertility is related to rather severe psychopathology in the woman, was based on clinical impressions. More systematic studies using the Rorschach (Eisner, 1963) and the Minnesota Multiphasic Personality Inventory (Carr, 1963) also reported more psychopathology among infertile than fertile wives. Nonetheless, the findings of a number of subsequent studies have been inconsistent with the view that infertility is caused by severe psychopathology (Denber & Roland, 1969; Hampson, 1963; Mai, Munday, & Rump, 1972a; Mattson, 1963; Richardson, 1972; Seward, 1965).

In infertility research to date, sex role identity generally has been viewed as an inherent personality characteristic of the woman rather than as a factor that may be environmentally affected. The lack of attention to social-psychological aspects of sex role and identity could partially explain the inconsistent findings in the infertility literature. Also, looking at sex role identity as a stable intrapsychic trait fails to account adequately for cases of secondary infertility (i.e., those in which pregnancy has occurred in the past, but not recently). If role conceptions are influenced by the woman's life situation at any given time, and if they can in turn influence her fertility, then it is not difficult to imagine that she might become infertile, temporarily or permanently, due to changed role demands and conflicts.

The difficulty of differentially diagnosing organic versus psychogenic infertility has been addressed by Mai, Munday, and Rump (1972b) and Decker (1972). Sandler's (1968) approach dealt with these problems by defining emotionally-based infertility as a somatic response to a state of stress rather than defining it in terms of the absence of demonstrable endocrine dysfunction or organic disease. McDonald (1968) has conceptualized the psychogenesis of obstetric complications in a similar fashion.

Beck (1972) has developed a model of psychophysiological disorders, positing the existence of an external situation that creates stress for the individual because of the meaning attached to it. Once the anxiety-provoking situation is established, the situational cues for anxiety, together with the symptoms of the physiological disorder, evoke additional anxiety; consequently, a "cognition-anxiety-physiological disorder" spiral is produced.

## Role Theory and Women's Roles

Role theory in general is concerned with the social context, rather than the individual in isolation, thus providing a clear contrast to those approaches to the psychology of women that have assumed a strong biological determinism and ignored social-psychological factors.

The phenomenon of women's ambivalence toward their roles

was examined from a role theory perspective by Rossi (1972), who stated that social roles always evoke ambivalence, but that when a role is optional, negative feelings about it are admissible. Because traditional women's roles (especially of wife and mother) have been required, ascribed roles, women's ambivalence toward them has been unacceptable and heavily sanctioned, creating guilt and other problems for women and their families. This ambivalence has physiological implications. There is evidence that if an individual is unable to resolve a role conflict, role performance is impaired and somatic disorders may result (Jackson, 1962; Sarbin & Allen, 1968).

In the growing body of literature on "psychological androgyny," there is increasing evidence that the stereotypically sex-typed woman (or man) has a narrower range of functioning than the androgynous individual. Moreover, sex-typed individuals have been found to rank lower in self-esteem and higher in anxiety, and to be sick more often than their androgynous counterparts (Bem, 1975; Bem, Martyna, & Watson, 1976; Deaux, 1976).

Factors associated with differences in degree of role conflict include marital status (Nevill & Damico, 1975) and husband's role expectations for his wife (Stuckert, 1962; Arnott, 1972). Women who are employed, especially in higher-level positions, face particular conflicts between traditional role expectations and the role of the working person (Bass, Krusell, & Alexander, 1971; Epstein, 1970; Gordon & Hall, 1974; Hall & Gordon, 1973). This is more of a problem for married women with a more traditional sex-based division of labor in the household (Markus, 1970).

## Women's Roles as Related to Fertility/Infertility

Most researchers exploring the relationship of women's roles and role conflict to fertility/infertility have been concerned only with consciously chosen fertility, with the exception of Safilios-Rothschild (1972). In general, the research has revealed that high work commitment is correlated with low fertility (Beckman, 1974; Harmon, 1970; Hass, 1972; Safilios-Rothschild, 1972; Weller, 1968). A study by Vogel, Rosenkrantz, Broverman, Broverman, & Clarkson (1975) indicated that women with less stereotypic sex-role conceptions wish to have fewer children.

For women who hold a traditional view of women's roles, any expectations or needs that conflict with the traditional maternal role may be stressful, increasing the likelihood of a somatic response. But a somatic response to stress is not necessarily dysfunctional. In some situations a physiological response can be more adaptive than the lack of autonomic involvement (Kagan & Moss, 1962; Lacey, 1967; Schacter, Williams, Rowe, Schacter, & Jameson, 1965). More specifically, infertility may have behaviorally adaptive significance in the transactions of the individual with her/his environment.

For example, Mead (1958) found that Samoan girls normally are sexually promiscuous before marriage but rarely become pregnant. They manifest a kind of temporary, functional infertility that is in no way a disease entity within their phenomenological and social context. In their culture, girls are expected to be sexually active, but they are not considered ready for motherhood. Infertility obviously functions differently in the cultural context of married American women than it does for Samoan girls. Nonetheless, the Samoan example suggests the possibility that infertility could be functional in our society as well.

## Hypotheses

This study was designed to explore the notion that infertility may be a somatic correlate to the stress of role conflict. More specifically, it was predicted that the lives of infertile women would display sources of role conflict, but that their perception of role conflict would be minimized. The following hypotheses were generated:

1. *Infertile women's views of themselves will include more traditional women's role conceptions than those of women in the comparison group.* Evidence from androgyny studies cited above suggests that traditionally sex-typed women are more restricted in their functioning, more anxious, and more illness-prone than women with less strictly traditional views of themselves.

2. *Infertile women will display greater discrepancy than comparison group women on the following measures: (a) "real self" role conceptions versus "ideal woman" role expectations; (b) "real self" role conceptions versus their perception of "man's ideal woman" role expectations; (c) "ideal woman" role expectations versus perceptions of "man's ideal woman" role expectations; (d) total internal role discrepancy.*

3. *Infertile couples will display more discrepancy than comparison group couples on the following: (a) wife's "real self" role conceptions versus husband's "ideal woman" role expectations; (b) wife's perception of "man's ideal woman" role expectations versus hus-*

band's actual "ideal woman" role expectations. These discrepancies would demonstrate conflict of role expectations between wife and husband.

4. *Infertile women will report less perceived conflict than comparison group women in the following areas: (a) child care (for women with children only); (b) relations with husband; (c) household management; (d) roles as women overall.* In other words, an infertile woman would *perceive* herself to be relatively unconflicted if infertility is functional in reducing the woman's *experience* of role conflict (which she is unable to resolve in any other fashion).

5. *In the area of occupation: (a) more infertile women than comparison group women will be employed; (b) infertile women's occupational status will be higher than that of comparison group women; (c) more infertile women than comparison group women will have had mothers who were employed; (d) infertile women will have had mothers who had higher occupational status than comparison group women's mothers.* The first two parts are based directly on Safilios-Rothschild's (1972) findings. Predictions regarding mothers' work commitment were based on the rationale that the role model provided by a mother with a work commitment would be another source of role conflict with the traditional role conceptions predicted in the first hypothesis.

## METHOD

### Subjects

The infertile subjects in the study were 29 women between ages 21 and 40 who, with their husbands, were beginning an infertility program at a private medical clinic in Los Angeles. To begin the program, a couple must have engaged in intercourse, without using contraception and without conceiving a pregnancy, for at least 12 months.

Comparison group subjects consisted of 29 married women, in the same age range and from comparable socio-economic areas, who had no history of inability to conceive pregnancy. Six of them were found through a dentist's office near the infertility clinic; married patients were approached, the nature of the study briefly explained, and their participation requested. The other control subjects were found through a "grapevine" procedure, in which each comparison subject was asked whether she could suggest other potential participants. All subjects signed voluntary consent forms for anonymous use of all relevant data for research. The two groups were comparable on demographic variables of age, family's income bracket, level of education, and religion, although there was a non-significant trend toward more Catholicism among the infertile group ($p<.10$).

## Procedures

After cooperation was obtained, each subject was asked to complete three Maferr Inventories of Feminine Values (Steinmann and Fox, 1974), from which role conceptions and expectations were measured. Each husband was also asked to complete a fourth Maferr Inventory. Each Inventory contains 34 statements, to be rated on a 5-point Likert scale of agreement. Half of the statements delineate "family-oriented" or traditional women's role conceptions, and half are "self-achieving" or non-traditional. Form A measures the woman's "real self" role conceptions; Form B asks how her "ideal woman" would respond. The husband's form, BB, indicates his role expectations for his "ideal woman." Role discrepancy scores were obtained by computing discrepancies between various pairs of scores, so that A minus B, for example, measures the woman's discrepancy between her perceptions of "real" versus "ideal self" role conceptions. The woman's total internal role discrepancy score was obtained by summing the absolute values of the discrepancy scores involving only the wife's forms (A, B, and C).

A Life Style Questionnaire, measuring experienced role conflict in several areas (Nevill & Damico, 1974), and a medical history questionnaire, developed and used routinely by the clinic, were also completed by each woman. The latter contained demographic information and some medical history to follow up in the interview.

Finally, a semi-structured interview was conducted with each subject, which was designed to explore the woman's experience and view of herself, with particular emphasis on the meaning of pregnancy and parenthood, and role conceptions and conflicts. Areas of focus included demographic variables, attitudes, motivations and experience related to pregnancy and having children, the marriage, the woman's parents and childhood experience, her view of herself, and possible role conflict. Due to space limitations, discussion of the interview material is beyond the scope of this paper, however.

## RESULTS

### Data Analysis

Statistical findings supported the hypotheses dealing with the women's role conceptions, self-reported role conflict, and occupational data. Significant differences between the infertile and comparison groups were found in the opposite direction from those predicted with regard to the women's internal role discrepancies.

*Women's role conceptions.* With regard to the first hypothesis, as Table 1 indicates, the ranked scores for "woman's view of herself" for the infertile sample are significantly lower than those for the comparison group ($p<.005$). The infertile group's scores on "woman's ideal woman" are also significantly lower than those of the comparison group ($p<.005$). In other words, as predicted, infertile women see not only themselves, but also their ideal woman, as significantly more traditional than do control group women.

*Role discrepancies.* Hypotheses 2 and 3 were tested by Mann-Whitney U comparisons of the absolute values of discrepancy scores. Absolute values were used because the discrepancies could emerge as either a positive or a negative value, with a score of zero representing no discrepancy. In Table 2, the findings are summarized, including non-absolute-value median scores to indicate the direction of the discrepancies.

Hypothesis 2, that infertile women would display more role discrepancy than comparison group women, was not supported. In fact, the findings were in the *opposite* direction from those predicted, with

Table 1

Mann-Whitney U-test Comparisons of

Maferr Inventory Scores

| Inventory | Infertile group ($\underline{n}$ = 29) | | Comparison group ($\underline{n}$ = 29) | | |
|---|---|---|---|---|---|
| | Median score | Mean $\underline{R}$ | Median score | Mean $\underline{R}$ | $\underline{U}$ |
| A: Woman's real self | 2 | 22.41 | 14 | 36.59 | 10.21*** |
| B: Woman's ideal woman | 6 | 22.91 | 20 | 36.09 | 8.82*** |
| C: Woman's perception of man's ideal woman | -4 | 29.41 | -4 | 29.59 | .001 |
| BB: Husband's ideal woman | 10 | 28.71 | 10 | 30.29 | .13 |

***$\underline{p}$ < .005

Table 2

Mann-Whitney U-test Comparisons of

Maferr Role Discrepancy Scores

| Role discrepancy variable | Infertile group (n = 29) | | Comparison group (n = 29) | | |
|---|---|---|---|---|---|
| | Median discrepancy | Mean R | Median discrepancy | Mean R | U |
| A- B: Real self vs. ideal woman | -3 | 25.72 | -4 | 33.82 | 2.90 |
| A - C: Real self vs. perception of man's ideal woman | 7 | 24.57 | 16 | 34.43 | 4.95* |
| B - C: Ideal woman vs. perception of man's ideal woman | 8 | 24.88 | 19 | 34.12 | 4.34* |
| $\|A - B\| + \|A - C\| + \|B - C\|$ : Total internal role discrepancy | 26 | 23.43 | 42 | 35.57 | 7.49** |
| A - BB: Real self vs. husband's ideal woman | -7 | 30.76 | 3 | 28.84 | .32 |
| C - BB: Perception of man's ideal woman vs. husband's ideal woman | -23 | 28.00 | -19 | 31.00 | .46 |

Note: Absolute values of discrepancy scores were used for statis-

tical comparison.

*p < .05

**p < .01

the infertile group displaying *less* discrepancy than the comparison group between their view of themselves and their perception of what men want from a woman ($p<.05$), and less discrepancy between their own role expectations for their ideal woman and those they perceive men to hold ($p<.05$). The infertile group also displayed less total internal role discrepancy than comparison group subjects ($p<.01$).

PSYCHOLOGY OF WOMEN QUARTERLY

*Self-reported role conflict.* In Hypothesis 4, it was predicted that infertile women would report less perceived role conflict than comparison group women. All parts of this hypothesis were supported by Mann-Whitney U analysis of the data (see Table 3). (a) Infertile women with children reported significantly less ($p<.01$) perceived conflict in the area of child care than comparison group women with children. Infertile women also reported less perceived conflict than control women in (b) the area of relations with husband

Table 3

Mann-Whitney $\underline{U}$-test Comparisons of

Life Style Questionnaire Scores on Role Conflict Areas

| Conflict area | Infertile group ($\underline{n}$ = 29) | | Comparison group ($\underline{n}$ = 29) | | |
|---|---|---|---|---|---|
| | Median reported conflict | Mean $\underline{R}$ | Median reported conflict | Mean $\underline{R}$ | $\underline{U}$ |
| Time management | 3 | 24.12 | 5 | 34.88 | 5.89** |
| Relations with husband | 1 | 23.50 | 2 | 35.50 | 7.32** |
| Household management | 2 | 23.97 | 3 | 35.03 | 6.23* |
| Child care | 2 | 13.93[a] | 3.5 | 24.04[b] | 6.81** |
| Financial | 2 | 26.38 | 2 | 32.62 | 1.98 |
| Expectations for self | 3 | 25.95 | 5 | 33.05 | 2.57 |
| Expectations from others | 2 | 28.93 | 2 | 30.07 | .07 |
| Guilt | 2 | 26.79 | 3 | 32.21 | 1.49 |
| Total reported role conflict, excluding child care item | 18 | 24.34 | 23 | 34.66 | 5.41* |
| Total reported role conflict, including child care item | 19 | 13.42[a] | 27 | 24.29[b] | 7.80*** |

Note: Scores are subjects' ratings from 1 (least conflict) to 7 (most conflict).

[a] $\underline{n}$ = 14

[b] $\underline{n}$ = 26

*$\underline{p}$ <.05

**$\underline{p}$ <.01

***$\underline{p}$ < .005

Table 4

Chi-square Comparisons of

Frequency of Employment

| Variable | Infertile group ($\underline{n}$ = 29) | | Comparison group ($\underline{n}$ = 29) | | $\underline{\chi}^2$ |
|---|---|---|---|---|---|
| | Freq. | % | Freq. | % | |
| Employment of subject | 18 | 62.07 | 8 | 27.59 | 5.65* |
| Employment of subject's mother | 9 | 31.03 | 5 | 17.24 | .85 |

*$\underline{p}$ < .05

($p<.05$), and (c) in the area of household management ($p<.05$). (d) The last part of this hypothesis was tested in two different ways. First, when a comparison of all women in both samples was made (excluding the "child care" conflict item, because of the number of subjects who had no children), infertile women showed less ($p<.05$) total reported role conflict than the control women. When a second comparison looked at only women with children (now including all of the self-reported role conflict items), the difference between infertile and control group women was even more significant ($p<.005$).

*Occupational involvement.* The fifth hypothesis was tested by comparing occupational data collected in the interview, with results summarized in Tables 4 and 5. Parts 5a and 5b were supported by the data, indicating that significantly more infertile women were employed ($p<.05$), and at significantly higher occupational statuses than comparison group women ($p<.05$). Parts 5c and 5d were not confirmed.

## DISCUSSION

The findings indicate that the infertile women have significantly more traditional role conceptions than the comparison group, and

Table 5

Mann-Whitney U-test Comparisons

of Occupational Status

| Variable | Infertile group (n = 29) | | Comparison group (n = 29) | | |
|---|---|---|---|---|---|
| | Median | Mean R | Median | Mean R | U |
| Occupational status of subject | 4 | 24.09 | 8 | 34.91 | 5.96* |
| Occupational status of subject's mother | 8 | 27.52 | 8 | 31.48 | .80 |

*p < .05

Note. Occupational status was coded according to the following adaptation of Hollingshead's (Note 4) scale:

  1 = Higher executives, proprietors of large concerns, major professionals

  2 = Business managers, proprietors of medium-sized businesses, lesser professionals

  3 = Administrative personnel, small independent businesses, minor professionals

  4 = Clerical and sales workers, technicians, owners of little businesses

  5 = Skilled manual workers

  6 = Machine operators and semi-skilled employees

  7 = Unskilled employees

  8 = No employment--housewives

that they consistently report less internally experienced role conflict than comparison group women. There is evidence, however, that the infertile women are and have been confronted with situations that could be expected to generate role conflict. Their levels of wife-husband role discrepancy are at least as high as those of the control group, and their higher levels of employment and occupational status seem to contradict their more traditional role conceptions.

One explanation for these findings is that the discrepancy between the traditional role conceptions of infertile subjects (with childbearing as a major element) and their inability to perform the childbearing function leads them to focus even more on their desire to have children and be traditional (which of course also intensifies the discrepancy).

It may also be that the traditional role conceptions actually contribute in some way to the infertility. For some infertile women, the ascribed, nonoptional nature of their traditional role conceptions (including childbearing) may somehow interfere with the conditions needed for conception to occur. As noted earlier, Rossi (1972) has argued that traditionally wifehood and motherhood are required, ascribed roles for women, and that therefore any ambivalence is unacceptance and tends to become covert, creating guilt and other negative consequences. Infertility might be one such possible consequence for women who hold nonoptional role expectations of childbearing, especially if they have cause for ambivalence about that role.

How, then, do the role conflict data fit into this emerging configuration? Infertility, in this sample, is associated with a greater traditionalism in the woman's role conceptions, which is consistent with the demands of woman's traditionally ascribed, nonoptional roles. If, as suggested above, infertility itself contributes to such traditionalism, and if such traditionalism suppresses ambivalence or conflict around their roles as women, then it follows that infertility functions indirectly to minimize the experience of role conflict.

The role discrepancy findings suggest that the infertile women's traditionalism functions to decrease the discrepancy between their own role conceptions and those that they perceive men to hold for them. It is the traditionalism that distinguishes the infertile group from the control group. Women's perception of "man's ideal woman" is almost the same between the two groups. It may be that the infertile women deny certain of their own individual, "self-achieving" needs, in an attempt to meet men's expectations as they perceive them. If this is true, then, infertility may also function as a somatic expression of the unmet personal, self-achieving needs that cannot be satisfied in their highly traditional women's role structure. The somatic reality of infertility is perhaps more tolerable for these women than the experience of role conflict.

Although infertile women hold more traditional role conceptions, perhaps partially in response to their perception of what men want, the discrepancy data including husbands' own "ideal woman" role expectations indicates that the women actually have moved to a position more traditional than that which their husbands report they want. They are at least as discrepant from their husbands' self-reported expectations as the comparison group women are, but, unlike the comparison group, the infertile women do not reflect this wife-husband discrepancy in their *experience* of role conflict. This may be an example of a role-related pressure or conflict that is somatically expressed in their failure to conceive, rather than being experienced as a conflict of expectations. Of course, it could be that in some cases it is the husband himself who prevents conception.

Another source of potential role conflict for these women is a higher level of employment and occupational status, which is in distinct contrast with their significantly more traditional role conceptions.

Thus, it is suggested that the infertile woman is confronted with certain sources of potential role conflict, in an experiential context that makes the experience of role conflict intolerable. In part, this context consists of her already traditional role conceptions, which have an ascribed, nonoptional character. Infertility acts to remove the mother role from the arena of choice, which minimizes internal conflict in that area, since the woman can wholeheartedly *want* to fill the traditional role by having children. The more she is unable to do so, the more she is likely to want to do so, and this circular interaction becomes stabilized.

## Limitations and Suggestions for Further Research

Since this exploratory study does not follow a true experimental design, the conclusions must be considered suggestive. Two methodological limitations are particularly noteworthy.

In this study, the infertile group consists only of infertile women who are seriously seeking pregnancy. The model for understanding infertility phenomenologically would certainly be at least somewhat different for women who do not want or are uninterested in having children.

Another consideration is that the infertile and comparison samples were not randomly selected groups, although they were not found to be statistically different on the demographic variables tested. One difference between the two samples was a far greater refusal rate among potential comparison subjects, probably attributable to the fact that the study was germane to the central concern for the infertile group while they were at the clinic.

The development of an instrument that quantifies and measures sources of role conflict is needed. This would preferably be a phenomenologically oriented instrument, so that researchers could base conclusions on the woman's own experiential context.

More research is needed on the role of the husband in infertility. A complete and sophisticated understanding of infertility would involve an understanding of each partner and of their interaction.

Finally, further research is needed concerning psychological interventions with infertile women or couples, in light of the relationship found here between role conceptions and conflict and infertility. If infertility is part of a coping system for these women, intervention should proceed with caution and should reflect an awareness of the interaction of the biological and social-psychological variables involved.

## REFERENCES

Arnott, C. C. Husbands' and wives' commitment to employment. *Journal of Marriage and the Family*, 1972, *34*, 673–684.

Bardwick, J. M. *The psychology of women: A study of bio-cultural conflicts.* New York: Harper & Row, 1971.

Bardwick, J. M., & Douvan, E. Ambivalence: The socialization of women. In V. Gornick & B. K. Moran (Eds.), *Woman in sexist society: Studies in power and powerlessness.* New York: Basic Books, 1971.

Bass, B. M., Krusell, J., & Alexander, R. A. Male managers' attitudes toward working women. *American Behavioral Scientist,* 1971, *15,* 221–236.

Beck, A. T. Cognition, anxiety, and psychophysiological disorders. In C. D. Spielberger (Ed.), *Anxiety—current trends in theory and research* (Vol. 2). New York: Academic Press, 1972.

Beckman, L. J. *Women's fertility, motivation for parenthood and work force participation.* Paper presented at the University of Oregon Psychology Department Colloquium, May 1974.

Bem, S. L. Sex-role adaptability: One consequence of psychological androgyny. *Journal of Personality and Social Psychology,* 1975, *31,* 634–643.

Bem, S. L., Martyna, W., & Watson, C. Sex typing and androgyny: Further explorations of the expressive domain. *Journal of Personality and Social Psychology,* 1976, *34,* 1016–1023.

Benedek, T., & Rubenstein, B. B. The correlation between ovarian activity and psychodynamic processes: I. The ovulative phase. *Psychosomatic Medicine,* 1939, *1,* 245–270.

Benedek, T. The psychobiology of pregnancy. In E. J. Anthony & T. Benedek (Eds.), *Parenthood, its psychology and psychopathology.* Boston: Little, Brown & Company, 1970.

Carr, G. D. *A psychosociological study of fertile and infertile marriages.* Unpublished doctoral dissertation, University of Southern California, 1963.

Carr, G. D. *A psychosociological study of fertile and infertile marriages.* Unpublished doctoral dissertation, University of Southern California, 1963.

Clifford, E. Expressed attitudes in pregnancies of unwed women and married primigravida and multigravida. *Child Development,* 1962, *33,* 945–951.

Deaux, K. *The behavior of women and men.* Monterey, Calif.: Brook/Cole, 1976.

Decker, A. Psychogenic infertility: Fact or fiction? *Medical Aspects of Human Sexuality,* 1972, *6,* 168–175.

Denber, H., & Roland, M. Psychologic factors and infertility. *Journal of Reproductive Medicine,* 1969, *2,* 29–34.

Deutsch, H. *The psychology of women* (2 vols.). New York: Grune & Stratton, 1944, 1945.

Eisner, B. G. Some psychological differences between fertile and infertile women. *Journal of Clinical Psychology,* 1963, *19,* 391–395.

Epstein, C. F. *Woman's place: Options and limits in professional careers.* Berkeley: University of California Press, 1970.

Ford, E. S. C., Forman, I., Wilson, J. R., Char, W., Mixson, W. T., & Scholz, C. A psychosomatic approach to the study of infertility. *Fertility & Sterility,* 1953, *6,* 456–465.

PSYCHOLOGY OF WOMEN QUARTERLY

Freud, S. Female sexuality. In J. Strachey (Ed. and trans.), *Collected papers* (Vol. 5). New York: Basic Books, 1959 (Originally published in 1931). (a)

Freud, S. Some psychological consequences of the anatomical distinction between the sexes. In J. Strachey (Ed. and trans.), *Collected papers* (Vol. 5). New York: Basic Books, 1959 (Originally published in 1925.) (b)

Gordon, F. E., & Hall, D. T. Self-image and stereotypes of femininity: Their relationship to women's role conflicts and coping. *Journal of Applied Psychology*, 1974, *59*, 241–243.

Greenberg, N. H., Loesch, J. G., & Lakin, M. Life situations associated with the onset of pregnancy—1. The role of separation in a group of unmarried pregnant women. *Psychosomatic Medicine*, 1959, *21*, 296–310.

Hall, D. T., & Gordon, F. E. Career choices of married women: Effects on conflict, role behavior and satisfaction. *Journal of Applied Psychology*, 1973, *58*, 42–48.

Hampson, J. L. *Objective personality studies of infertile couples.* Unpublished manuscript, University of Washington School of Medicine, 1963.

Harmon, L. Anatomy of career commitment in women. *Journal of Counseling Psychology*, 1970, *16*, 77–80.

Hass, P. H. Maternal role incompatibility and fertility in urban Latin America. *Journal of Social Issues*, 1972, *28*, 111–127.

Hatcher, L. M. The adolescent experience of pregnancy and abortion: A developmental analysis (Doctoral dissertation, University of Michigan, 1972). *Dissertation Abstracts International*, 1973, *34*, 4507B-4508B.

Hollingshead, A. B. *Two-factor index of social position.* Unpublished manuscript, 1957. (Available from 1965 Yale Station, New Haven, Connecticut.)

Jackson, E. F. Status consistency and symptoms of stress. *American Sociological Review*, 1962, *27*, 469–480.

Jones, B. The dynamics of marriage and motherhood. In R. Morgan (Ed.), *Sisterhood is powerful.* New York: Vintage, 1970.

Kagan, J., & Moss, H. A. *Birth to maturity.* New York: Wiley, 1962.

Lacey, J. I. Somatic response patterning and stress: Some revisions of activation theory. In M. H. Appley & R. Trumbull (Eds.), *Psychological stress.* New York: Appleton-Century-Crofts, 1967.

Lott, B. E. Who wants the children? Some relationships among attitudes toward children, parents, and the liberation of women. *American Psychologist*, 1973, *28*, 573–582.

Mai, F. M., Munday, R. N., & Rump, E. E. Psychiatric interview comparisons between infertile and fertile couples. *Psychosomatic Medicine*, 1972, *34*, 431–440. (a)

Mai, F. M., Munday, R. N., & Rump, E. E. Psychosomatic and behavioral mechanisms in psychogenic infertility. *British Journal of Psychiatry*, 1972, *120*, 199–204. (b)

Mandy, T. E., & Mandy, A. J. The psychosomatic aspects of infertility. *International Journal of Fertility*, 1958, *3*, 287–295.

Markus, M. Women and work: Feminine emancipation at an impasse. *Impact of Science on Society*, 1970, *20*, 61–72.

Mattson, M. R. *Objective personality studies of psychogenically infertile women.* Unpublished manuscript, University of Washington School of Medicine, 1963.

McDonald, R. L. The role of emotional factors in obstetric complications: A review. *Psychosomatic Medicine*, 1968, *30*, 222–237.

Mead, M. Adolescence in primitive and modern society. In E. E. Maccoby, T. M. Newcomb & E. L. Hartley (Eds.), *Readings in social psychology.* New York: Holt, Rinehart & Winston, 1958.

Mitchell, J. *Woman's estate.* New York: Vintage, 1973.

Nevill, D., & Damico, S. The development of a role conflict questionnaire for women: Some preliminary findings. *Journal of Consulting and Clinical Psychology*, 1974, *42*, 743.

Nevill, D., & Damico, S. Role conflict in women as a function of marital status. *Human Relations*, 1975, *28*, 478–498.

Noyes, R. W., & Chapnick, E. M. Literature on psychology and infertility—A critical analysis. *Fertility and Sterility*, 1964, *15*, 543–558.

Richardson, I. M. A comparative study of personality characteristics of functionally infertile and fertile women (Doctoral dissertation, Texas Technical University, 1972). *Dissertation Abstracts International,* 1972, *33,* 2772A-2773A.

Rossi, A. S. The roots of ambivalence in American women. In J. M. Bardwick (Ed.), *Readings on the psychology of women.* New York: Harper & Row, 1972.

Russo, N. F. The motherhood mandate. *Journal of Social Issues,* 1976, *32,* 143–153.

Safilios-Rothschild, C. The relationship between work commitment and fertility. *International Journal of Sociology of the Family,* 1972, *2,* 64–71.

Sandler, B. Emotional stress and infertility. *Journal of Psychosomatic Research,* 1968, *12,* 51–59.

Sarbin, T. R., & Allen, V. L. Role theory. In G. Lindzey & E. Aronson (Eds.), *The handbook of social psychology* (2nd ed., Vol. 1). Reading, Mass.: Addison-Wesley Publishing Company, 1968.

Schacter, J., Williams, T. A., Rowe, R., Schacter, J. S., & Jameson, J. Personality correlates of physiological reactivity to stress: A study of 46 college males. *American Journal of Psychiatry,* 1965, *121,* 12–24.

Seward, G. H., Wagner, P. S., Heinrich, J. F., Bloch, S. K., & Myerhoff, H. L. The question of psychophysiologic infertility: Some negative answers. *Psychosomatic Medicine,* 1965, *27,* 533–547.

Steinmann, A., & Fox, D. J. *The male dilemma.* New York: Jason Aronson, Inc., 1974.

Stuckert, R. P. Role perception and marital satisfaction—A configurational approach. *Marriage and Family Living,* 1963, *25,* 415–419.

Vogel, S. R., Rosenkrantz, P. S., Broverman, D. M., & Clarkson, F. E. Sex-role self-concepts and life-style plans of young women. *Journal of Counseling and Clinical Psychology,* 1975, *43,* 427.

Weller, R. H. The employment of wives, dominance, and fertility. *Journal of Marriage and the Family,* 1968, *30,* 437–442.

# The Myth of Motherhood:
# A Study of Attitudes Toward Motherhood

Rachel T. Hare-Mustin and Patricia C. Broderick

*Villanova University*

Traditional attitudes toward motherhood reflect many contradictions. The Motherhood Inventory (MI), a 40 item questionnaire, has been developed to study attitudes toward motherhood and the motherhood myth. The MI includes items relating to the control of reproduction, abortion, adoption, single motherhood, male-female relationships, and idealized and punitive attitudes toward mothers. The 301 subjects in this study were drawn largely from undergraduate and graduate students at an eastern university and their parents. Comparisons with scores on the Spence-Helmreich Attitudes toward Women Scale (AWS) revealed that the sample was more liberal than the original AWS sample. Men were found to hold significantly more traditional attitudes toward motherhood than women. Younger subjects also agreed more with the myth of motherhood as did unmarried subjects. Catholics more than non-Catholics rejected abortion and supported the primacy of the woman's role as mother. Education produced the most pronounced effect on attitudes toward motherhood with more liberal attitudes held by those who were college graduates.

Although recent research has focused on attitudes toward women in their more liberated roles (Blanchard, Becker, & Bristow, 1976; Spence & Helmreich, 1972), there has yet to be a major study of attitudes toward motherhood. The fact that attitudes toward motherhood, that most sacrosanct and idealized of women's roles, may not have kept pace with attitude changes toward women's other roles reflects the conflicting ideas which have been part of the myth of motherhood.

Presented at the meeting of the American Psychological Association Toronto, August 1978. Reprint requests should be directed to Rachel T. Hare-Mustin 715 Brooke Rd. Wayne, PA. 19087.

*Psychology of Women Quarterly, Vol. 4(1) Fall 1979*
0361-6843/79/1500-0114$00.95 © 1979 Human Sciences Press

RACHEL T. HARE–MUSTIN AND PATRICIA C. BRODERICK

Society is now beginning to promote the rights of women to receive equal pay for their work, but this right somehow does not apply to the housewife and mother. Her "right" is to have children and to stay at home to raise them (Russo, 1976), and she is responsible for how they turn out (Abramowitz, 1977; Hare-Mustin, 1978). Although women may work, the common view is that their jobs should be subservient to their principal child bearing/rearing function. It is not surprising that the vast majority of American working women (70%) are in fields that conflict least with this essential role, viz. teaching, nursing, social services, and secretarial work (Tangri, 1972). Having children continues to be promoted as completely fulfilling despite a few realistic appraisals of the hard work and problems involved in mothering (Bernard, 1974; Minturn & Lambert, 1964; Rollin, 1970).

A review of recent literature on motherhood reveals the wealth of contradictory themes that create a myth of motherhood. For example, Blumenthal (1975), in arguing that the duties and burdens of motherhood have been stressed over its pleasures, claims that having a child gives a girl (sic) emotional security, that men are attracted to women because of their maternal capacity, that "sex was never meant to be enjoyed independently of the price humans were expected to pay for it" (p. 107). Rich (1976) points out that the idea of the mother is associated first with power, and only secondarily with warmth, that motherhood is so idealized that all mothers are more or less guilty of having failed their children, that a woman's love for her children comes before her love for her mate. Lott (1973) observes that our culture holds childbearing and childrearing in low esteem. In Lidz's (1968) view, the sense of fulfillment for a wife comes only with the creation of a new life. McBride (1973) challenges the myth of motherhood, pointing out that motherhood represents man's projection of an ideal, a set of behaviors and hopes that no flesh and blood woman could ever meet.

Only a powerful myth could encompass as many conflicting ideals as the myth of motherhood does. The issue of the good mother versus the bad mother undoubtedly influences policy and practices related to procreation, breast feeding, abortion, adoption, child care, and the employment of women outside the home. One obvious disparity is that society's idealization of motherhood has not been extended to unwed mothers and mothers who give their children up for adoption. In adoption, the natural mother is often looked upon as promiscuous; subsequent attitudes toward the adopted child may be powerfully influenced by the suspicion that the child comes from "bad seed" (Toussieng, 1962). It appears that it is not motherhood that is idealized but only motherhood under patriarchy, that is, within the socially acceptable confines of marriage (Rich, 1976).

How widely is the myth of motherhood held? What are its various aspects? Recent research on the psychology of women has examined attitudes toward women and their roles (Spence & Helmreich, 1972), but has not examined in detail attitudes toward motherhood itself. The present study reports the initial development of the Motherhood Inventory (MI) and the relation of liberal and traditional attitudes toward women to attitudes toward motherhood.

## METHOD

### Subjects

The 301 subjects included 177 females and 124 males, undergraduate and graduate students at an eastern university and their parents. Ages ranged from 17 to 69, with a mean of 29 ($SD = 12.28$). Religious preferences indicated 66% Catholic, 14% Protestant, 9% Jewish, 7% no religion, and 3% other. Forty percent of the subjects were married. Thirty-one percent had children. Of those with children, the mean number was 3.7 children which probably reflects the high proportion of Catholics in the sample. Age and sex were not significantly associated, but age and religion were, with the younger group more likely to be Catholic ($r = .30$). The Catholic group tended to have less education ($r = .42$), which could be a function of their being younger, since age and education were highly associated ($r = .68$). Married subjects tended to be older ($r = .76$), to have more education ($r = .45$), and to be Catholic ($r = .27$).

### Instruments

A short (25-item) version of the Spence-Helmreich Attitudes toward Women Scale (AWS) was used to assess the degree to which the subjects held traditional or liberal views toward women (Spence, Helmreich & Stapp, 1973). The short form consists of 25 statements that describe attitudes toward the role of women in society. Subjects respond in a four point Likert style with "agree strongly," "agree mildly," "disagree mildly," and "disagree strongly." Each item is given a score from 0 to 3, with 0 representing the most traditional and 3 the most contemporary, profeminist response. Scores are summed for a total score.

The Motherhood Inventory (MI) developed by the authors consists of 40 items to which the subjects respond as above. The initial item pool was generated from sentence completions to motherhood stems and reports of research on sex roles and mothering. The final items were based on responses by 12 judges and balanced for positive and negative direction. Topics included in the MI are decisions about having children, birth control, pregnancy, delivery, breast feeding, abortion, adoption, single motherhood, sexuality, promiscuity, child rearing responsibility, and personal fulfillment.

The Background Information Questionnaire included questions on age, sex, residence, religion, marital status, number of children, respondent's birth order, academic achievement, and job or professional status.

## Procedure

The subjects were given the Attitudes toward Women Scale followed by the Motherhood Inventory, and then the Background Information Question- naire. The materials were presented as one package using the instructions for the AWS with the MI items numbered sequentially beginning with item 26.

## RESULTS

### Relation of MI to AWS

The scores on the AWS ranged from 18 to 75 with a mean of 54.99 ($SD$ = 13.20). This mean is higher than the 44.80 for males and 50.26 for females at the University of Texas and the 39.22 and 41.86 for their fathers and mothers, respectively (Spence, Helmreich, & Stapp, 1973). Significant differences on the AWS were found for dif- ferent groups with females more liberal than males, older subjects more liberal than younger, college graduates more liberal than those with less than a college degree, and non-Catholics more liberal than Catholics. (Table 1.)

Responses to 32 of the 40 items on the MI correlated significantly with the AWS score ($p<.001$). The highest correlations ($r>.50$) indi- cated that the AWS profeminist score was negatively related to MI items on the idealization of motherhood such as:

A woman who doesn't want children is unnatural.

A woman who is true to her basic maternal instincts would not give a child up for adoption.

The true mission of women is the welfare of men and children.

If women want to be respected, they should try to be better mothers.

The reward for a mother is knowing she has done her duty.

Men must decide how far they will let women's liberation go.

Table 1

Mean Scores on the Attitudes toward Women Scale

| Group | $n^a$ | M | SD | t |
|---|---|---|---|---|
| Males | 116 | 47.52 | 12.69 | 9.17* |
| Females | 163 | 60.42 | 10.74 | |
| Younger (17-23) | 144 | 51.50 | 11.95 | 4.66* |
| Older (24-69) | 131 | 58.67 | 13.54 | |
| Undergraduate or less | 166 | 49.87 | 12.36 | 8.81* |
| College degree or post-college | 115 | 62.37 | 10.66 | |
| Catholic | 189 | 51.86 | 12.69 | 6.19* |
| Non-Catholic | 88 | 61.77 | 11.76 | |
| Unmarried | 173 | 53.11 | 11.76 | 3.27* |
| Married or formerly married | 105 | 58.36 | 14.83 | |

[a] Numbers vary due to some partial responses.

* $p < .001$, 2-tail

## Attitudes toward Motherhood

*Women's control over reproduction.* Responses to many of the items on birth control on the Motherhood Inventory were quite liberal; 86% felt that birth control information and services should be made available to all women. Almost all subjects (92%) indicated that women should have the right to withhold or initiate sexual activity within marriage. A majority (60%) did not agree that people should be guided by the teachings of religion in matters of sexual behavior. Half the subjects felt a woman had the right to have a child whether she was married or not.

Attitudes toward abortion tended to split the group. Only 13%

RACHEL T. HARE–MUSTIN AND PATRICIA C. BRODERICK

felt that any woman who would have an abortion must be unfit to be a good mother, but half the group felt that a woman should bear an unwanted child rather than have an abortion. Fifty-seven percent felt that it was natural for a woman to want an abortion if there were a fetal deformity. The same proportion recognized that legal abortion was safer than childbirth; 43% did not. In response to the statement that it should be the woman's right to decide about abortion without the man's permission, 39% agreed. This is at odds with the fact that 65% agreed with the more general principle, that a woman has the right to make the decision herself about having more children.

*Adoption.* Subjects felt that it was more acceptable to give up an unwanted child for adoption (61%) than have an abortion (49%). Furthermore, 64% thought that giving a child for adoption in no way indicated a failure to be true to one's basic maternal instincts. About half seemed to accept single motherhood since they did not agree that an unwed mother who gives her child for adoption rather than raising it alone demonstrates true caring for her child. As for attitudes toward adopted children, 31% felt adopted children came from poor unwed girls, 21% thought they were born out of wedlock, and 15% believed they were given for adoption because something was wrong with them.

*Punitive aspects of motherhood.* Almost half the subjects, 45%, agreed that women who wanted babies should be expected to pay for them in extra work and sacrifice. A similar proportion, 42%, felt that women who had abortions or gave their children up for adoption would always bear a heavy burden of guilt. A third of the subjects felt that if an unmarried woman got pregnant, it was her own fault. However, only 4% felt a single woman who became pregnant should marry a man she didn't love for the sake of the child. Twenty-one percent felt that being pregnant made a woman's body unattractive. Seventeen percent felt that if a woman died from an illegal abortion it was her own fault for wanting an abortion.

*Caring for men.* Most of the responses relating to men tended to be contemporary. Only 21% felt that women's true mission was the welfare of men and children. Half the subjects thought that it was the love and altruism of mothers that had made men's achievements possible. Conversely, a smaller percentage, 26%, thought that by taking responsibility for supporting women, men had made it easy for them. There were 18% who agreed that men must decide how far they will let women's liberation go.

*Women's identity and motherhood.* In general, there was a rejection of the idea that a woman's identity depended on her mothering functions. Approximately three quarters of the subjects disagreed that: the mother-child relationship is the essential human relationship, if women want to be respected they should try to be better mothers, and the true mission of women is the welfare of men and children, as mentioned above. Sixty-two percent disagreed that the reward for a mother was knowing she had done her duty.

*The myth of motherhood.* Attitudes toward the role of motherhood did not support the myth. Subjects overwhelmingly disagreed (88%) that the woman who did not want children was selfish or unnatural. Only 22% agreed with the idea that having a baby was totally fulfilling or that no child was unwanted for a normal woman. Half the subjects felt it was understandable that a mother might not like all her children, and 38% felt that most mothers were happiest once their children were in school. The realities of mothering were also reflected in the fact that three quarters of the group felt that motherhood was the hardest job there is. In terms of the physical aspects of motherhood, two-thirds of the sample felt that breast feeding was not acceptable in public. Clearly, breast feeding is a more widely held taboo than negative attitudes toward a pregnant woman's body which were held by 21%.

A majority (59%) agreed that most working mothers could raise their children as well as mothers who did not work. There was overwhelming rejection (87%) of the idea that a woman who does not have children should fulfill her maternal nature through teaching, nursing, social work, or similar occupation.

A third of the subjects said they would not want to grow up to be like their mothers.

## Differences in Attitudes by Age, Sex, Religion, Education, and Marital Status

The significance of such factors as age, sex, religion, education, and marital status was tested by use of chi square tests with the Yates correction. Reported differences are significant at $p<.001$ (1 $df$). No significant differences were found in responses for subjects with and without children, or on the basis of the respondent's birth order in his or her family of origin.

*Age and the motherhood myth.* The younger group (age 17–23) was much more accepting of the motherhood myth than the older

RACHEL T. HARE–MUSTIN AND PATRICIA C. BRODERICK

group (age 24–69). They were more likely to idealize the love and altruism of mothers, less likely to support a woman's right to an abortion, and more likely to see the reward for a mother as having done her duty. The older group seemed more realistic and tended to recognize that a mother might not like all her children. The older group was less likely to agree that motherhood was the hardest job there is. (See Figure 1.)

*Female/male attitudes.* Men's responses were much more conservative than women's as represented by the fact that 35% of the

THE MYTH OF MOTHERHOOD

    Motherhood is the hardest job

        there is

    The love and altruism of mothers

    makes men's achievements

    possible.

DECISIONS CONCERNING ABORTION

    A woman should have the right to

    abort without the man's

    permission.

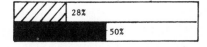

    It makes sense to abort rather than

    to bear an unwanted child.

PUNITIVE ASPECTS OF THE MYTH

    The reward for a mother is knowing

    she has done her duty.

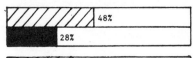

    It is understandable that a mother

    may not like all her children.

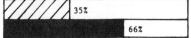

*Significant Differences: $p < .001$ (Chi square, 1 $df$)

Younger (Age 17–23) 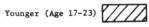    Older (Age 24–69)

FIGURE 1. Items showing significant differences in agreement by age*

men felt men must decide how far to let women's liberation go but only 5% of the women agreed. Men were more likely to feel that a woman who did not want children was unnatural and that women should be better mothers if they wanted to be respected. Men were less willing than women to allow women to control their reproduction. While a majority of the women felt that a working mother could raise her children as well as a mother who did not work, less than half the men agreed. (See Figure 2.)

THE MYTH OF MOTHERHOOD

Having a baby fulfills a woman totally.
32%
14%

A woman who doesn't want children is unnatural.
20%
6%

A truly maternal woman would not give up a child for adoption.
52%
24%

Women who want respect should be better mothers.
30%
13%

Working mothers can raise children as well as non-working mothers.
47%
68%

Men must decide how far women's liberation should go.
35%
5%

CONTROL OF REPRODUCTION

Women have the right to decide about having more children.
50%
75%

DECISIONS CONCERNING ABORTION

A woman should have the right to abort without the man's permission.
22%
50%

*Significant Differences: p < .001 (Chi square, 1 df)

Male ///////        Female ████

FIGURE 2. Items showing significant differences in agreement by sex*

RACHEL T. HARE–MUSTIN AND PATRICIA C. BRODERICK

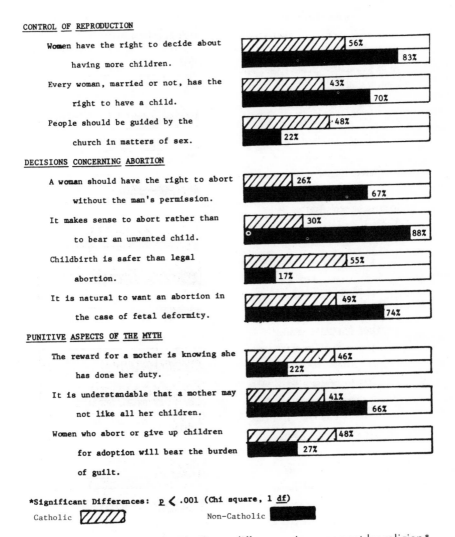

FIGURE 3. Items showing significant differences in agreement by religion*

*Religion and reproduction.* Significant differences between Catholics and non-Catholics were primarily in the area of a woman's right to control her reproduction. Only a quarter of the Catholics felt a woman had the right to decide about an abortion without the man's permission, compared with two-thirds of the non-Catholics. Slightly more Catholics felt that it was better to abort than to bear an unwanted child. Half the Catholics agreed it was natural to want to

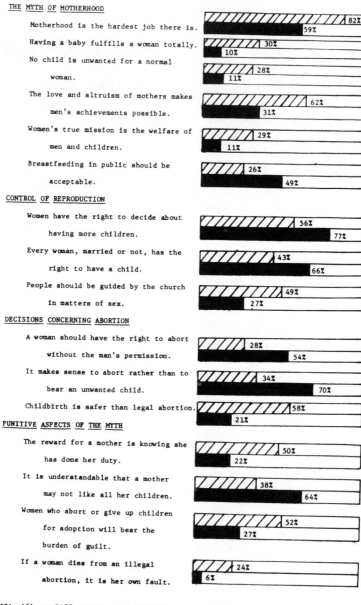

THE MYTH OF MOTHERHOOD

Motherhood is the hardest job there is. — 82% / 59%

Having a baby fulfills a woman totally. — 30% / 10%

No child is unwanted for a normal woman. — 28% / 11%

The love and altruism of mothers makes men's achievements possible. — 62% / 31%

Women's true mission is the welfare of men and children. — 29% / 11%

Breastfeeding in public should be acceptable. — 26% / 49%

CONTROL OF REPRODUCTION

Women have the right to decide about having more children. — 56% / 77%

Every woman, married or not, has the right to have a child. — 43% / 66%

People should be guided by the church in matters of sex. — 49% / 27%

DECISIONS CONCERNING ABORTION

A woman should have the right to abort without the man's permission. — 28% / 54%

It makes sense to abort rather than to bear an unwanted child. — 34% / 70%

Childbirth is safer than legal abortion. — 58% / 21%

PUNITIVE ASPECTS OF THE MYTH

The reward for a mother is knowing she has done her duty. — 50% / 22%

It is understandable that a mother may not like all her children. — 38% / 64%

Women who abort or give up children for adoption will bear the burden of guilt. — 52% / 27%

If a woman dies from an illegal abortion, it is her own fault. — 24% / 6%

*Significant Differences: $p < .001$ (Chi square, 1 df)

Less than college degree ////    College and post graduate degree ■

FIGURE 4. Items showing significant differences in agreement by education*

RACHEL T. HARE–MUSTIN AND PATRICIA C. BRODERICK

abort in the case of a fetal deformity, compared with three-quarters of the non-Catholics. More than half the Catholics thought childbirth was safer than legal abortion, while only a few of the non-Catholics did.

Almost half the Catholics felt people should be guided by religion in sexual matters and invoked duty and guilt in relation to motherhood, compared with less than a quarter of the non-Catholics. However, 43% of the Catholics felt every woman, whether married or not had a right to have a child. Seventy percent of the non-Catholics supported that right. (See Figure 3.)

*Education and attitudes toward motherhood.* Subjects currently in college or with less than a college degree were significantly more accepting of the motherhood myth than those who had graduated from college or had some post-college education. Less educated subjects were more likely to see motherhood as being totally fulfilling as well as the hardest job there is. They were less likely to find it understandable that a mother might not like all her children. In contrast, college graduates were more liberal about the woman's right to control her own reproduction than those without a college degree. More educated subjects were more likely to find breast feeding acceptable and were less punitive toward women who had abortions. Only a quarter of the college graduates felt religion should guide sexual matters compared with half of those with less education. (See Figure 4.)

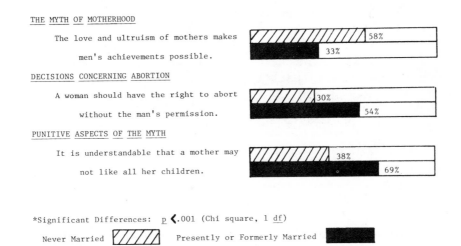

THE MYTH OF MOTHERHOOD

The love and ultruism of mothers makes men's achievements possible. — 58% / 33%

DECISIONS CONCERNING ABORTION

A woman should have the right to abort without the man's permission. — 30% / 54%

PUNITIVE ASPECTS OF THE MYTH

It is understandable that a mother may not like all her children. — 38% / 69%

*Significant Differences: $p < .001$ (Chi square, 1 df)

Never Married [////] Presently or Formerly Married [■■■]

FIGURE 5. Items showing significant differences in agreement by marital status*

*Marital status.* The few significant differences that were found between married or formerly married subjects and those never married indicated that married subjects were more liberal. Two thirds of the married group felt that it was understandable that a mother might not like all her children compared with a third of the unmarried group. More than half the married group thought a woman should have the right to decide on an abortion without the man's permission, but only one third of the unmarried did. Fifty-eight percent of the unmarried group felt that it was the love and altruism of mothers that made men's achievements possible, compared with a third of the never married group. (See Figure 5.)

## DISCUSSION

Responses to the MI were found to be generally liberal and indicated only slight support for the motherhood myth. Three fourths of the MI items correlated significantly with scores on the AWS.

The present study concurs with other studies using the AWS, in that women were generally found to be more liberal in their attitudes than were men. More conservative attitudes among male students were also found, not only at the University of Texas (Spence and Helmreich, 1972), but at the University of Washington (Lunneborg, 1974), and among students at the University of Calgary in Canada (Loo & Logan, 1977).

Most of the issues that divided men and women on the MI were concerned with power and decision-making; that is, the right to decide on an abortion, to have more children, and to work while raising children. The stereotype of the full-time housewife as a completely fulfilling role was more likely to be rejected by women than by men. A difference that did not reach the .001 level of significance, but is related, is that more males than females tended to agree with the statement that the mother-child relationship is the essential human relationship.

The expectation that younger subjects would hold more liberal attitudes toward motherhood was not supported. Older subjects were significantly more liberal, possibly because the experience of marriage and/or motherhood tempers to some extent the idealistic views which support the myth. The fact that most of the younger subjects were Catholic could also contribute to the conservatism of this age group. The younger group differed significantly from the older group in that they viewed motherhood in terms of a demanding but ultimately rewarding duty to be embraced altruistically in order to promote men's achievements.

The differences between Catholics and non-Catholics lay primarily in the area of sexuality and reproduction. Other studies have consistently shown Catholics to be more traditional on these issues than members of other religious groups (Bogen, 1974; Eagly & Anderson, 1974; Hedderson, Hodgson, Bogan, & Crowley, 1974; Richardson & Fox, 1975; Haskell, 1977). Catholic responses indicated a strong rejection of abortion and a firm acceptance of the role of women as primarily that of mother.

The greatest number of significant differences in attitudes occurred as a function of differences in levels of education. Generally, those with less education supported the "myth of motherhood" and were conservative on issues of sex and reproduction. This finding is congruent with other research that has found education to have the most pronounced effect on sex-role attitudes overall (Mason & Bumpass, 1970). Few differences were found based on marital status. Married or formerly married subjects were more liberal than those who had never been married.

The research reported here represents the initial development of a scale to study attitudes toward motherhood, the Motherhood Inventory. The findings reported indicate that there are significant differences in the way different groups respond to various aspects of motherhood.

## REFERENCES

Abramowitz, C. V. Blaming the mother: An experimental investigation of sex-role bias in countertransference. *Psychology of Women Quarterly*, 1977, *2*, 24–34.

Bernard, J. *The future of motherhood*. New York: Dial Press, 1974.

Blanchard, C. G., Becker, J. V., & Bristow, A. P., Attitudes of Southern women: Selected group comparisons. *Psychology of Women Quarterly*, 1976, *1*, 160–171.

Bogen, I. Attitudes of women who have had abortions. *Journal of Sex Research*, 1974, *10*, 97–109.

Blumenthal, S. L. *The retreat from motherhood*. New Rochelle, N.Y.: Arlington House, 1975.

Eagly, A., & Anderson, P. Sex role and attitudinal correlates of desired family size. *Journal of Applied Social Psychology*, 1974, *4*, 151–164.

Hare-Mustin, R. T. A feminist approach to family therapy. *Family Process*, 1978, *17*, 181–194.

Haskell, S. Desired family-size correlates for single undergraduates. *Psychology of Women Quarterly*, 1977, *2*, 5–15.

Hedderson, J., Hodgson, L., Bogan, M., & Crowley, T. Determinants of abortion attitudes in the United States in 1972. *Journal of Social Relations*, 1974, *9*, 261–276.

Lidz, T. The effects of children on marriage. In S. Rosenbaum & I. Alger (Eds.), *The marriage relationship: Psychoanalytic perspectives*. New York: Basic Books, 1968.

Loo, R., & Logan, P. Investigation of the Attitudes toward Women Scale in western Canada. *Canadian Journal of Behavioral Science*, 1977, *9*, 201–204.

Lott, B. E. Who wants children? Some relationships among attitudes toward children, parents, and the liberation of women. *American Psychologist,* 1973, *28,* 573–582.

Lunneborg, P. Validity of Attitudes toward Women Scale. *Psychological Reports,* 1974, *34,* 1281–1282.

Mason, K., & Bumpass, L. U.S. women's sex-role ideology. *American Journal of Sociology,* 1970, *80,* 1212–1219.

McBride, A. B. *The growth and development of mothers.* New York: Harper & Row, 1973.

Minturn, L, & Lambert, W. W. *Mothers of six cultures, antecedents of child rearing;* New York: Wiley, 1964.

Rich, A. *Of woman born.* New York: W. W. Norton, 1976.

Richardson, J., & Fox, S. Religion and voting on abortion reform: A follow-up study. *Journal for the Scientific Study of Religion,* 1975, *14,* 159–164.

Rollin, B. F. Motherhood: Who needs it? *Look,* September 22, 1970, 15–17.

Russo, N. The motherhood mandate. *Journal of Social Issues,* 1976, *32,* 143–153.

Spence, J. T., & Helmreich, R. The attitudes toward women scale: An objective instrument to measure attitudes toward the rights and roles of women in contemporary society. *JSAS Catalog of Selected Documents in Psychology,* 1972, *2,* 66.

Spence, J. T., Helmreich, R., & Stapp, J. A short version of the attitudes toward women scale (AWS). *Bulletin of the Psychonomic Society,* 1973, *2,* 219–220.

Tangri, S. S. Determinants of occupational role innovation among college women. *Journal of Social Issues,* 1972, *28,* 177–199.

Toussieng, P. Thoughts regarding the etiology of psychological difficulties in adopted children. *Child Welfare,* February 1962, 59–71.

# Book Reviews

THE BEHAVIOR OF WOMEN AND MEN. Kay Deaux. Monterey Calif.: Brooks/Cole, 1976, 168 pp., $4.95.

WOMEN: A PSYCHOLOGICAL PERSPECTIVE. Elaine Donelson and Jeanne Gullahorne. New York: John Wiley & Sons, 1977, 342 pp., $13.95.

SEX ROLES AND PERSONAL AWARENESS. Barbara Lusk Forisha. Morristown, N.J.: General Learning Press, 1978, 414 pp., $7.95.

WOMEN AND SEX ROLES: A SOCIAL PSYCHOLOGICAL PERSPECTIVE. Irene H. Frieze, Jacquelynne E. Parsons, Paula B. Johnson, Diane N. Ruble, Gail L. Zellman. New York: W. W. Norton Co., 1978, 444 pp., $13.95.

HALF THE HUMAN EXPERIENCE: THE PSYCHOLOGY OF WOMEN. Janet Shibley Hyde and B. G. Rosenberg. Lexington, Mass.: D. C. Heath & Co., 1976, 306 pp., $5.95.

TOWARD UNDERSTANDING WOMEN. Virginia E. O'Leary. Monterey, California: Brooks/Cole, 1977, 253 pp., $8.95.

THE LONGEST WAR: SEX DIFFERENCES IN PERSPECTIVE. Carol Tavris and Carole Offir. New York: Harcourt, Brace, Jovanovich, 1977, 333 pp., $6.95.

SEX ROLES: BIOLOGICAL, PSYCHOLOGICAL, AND SOCIAL FOUNDATIONS. Shirley Weitz. New York: Oxford University Press, 1977, 283 pp., $4.95.

SEX-ROLE PSYCHOLOGY. Frank Wesley and Claire Wesley. New York: Human Sciences Press, 1977, 224 pp., $6.95.

PSYCHOLOGY OF WOMEN: BEHAVIOR IN A BIOSOCIAL CONTEXT. Juanita H. Williams. New York: W. W. Norton & Co., 1977, 444 pp., $9.95.

A sure sign that a new academic field has gained acceptance is the appearance of a healthy crop of textbooks. By this criterion, the psychology of women has recently come of age. In the past few years, a large number of textbooks on this topic have been published. In this brief review, we examine ten new texts published in 1976 or more recently. We consider the emerging conception of the field reflected in these books, present a quick "reader's guide" to the texts, and add a few thoughts about future directions in this area.

## An Emerging Conception of the Field

An important function of textbooks is to define and shape new academic fields. As represented in these ten books, the psychology of women is a vital and growing field. We agree with O'Leary that "Psychologists have learned more about the behavior and experience of women and girls in the last decade than they had in the previous six" (p. 202). New textbooks present scholarly reviews of research and theory, and demonstrate that a clearer understanding of women is crucial to understanding human behavior in general. The new crop of books should also refute criticisms that the psychology of women as an area lacks scholarly substance.

Although the ten books we reviewed are diverse, they suggest an emerging consensus about core topics in the psychology of women. With few exceptions, all texts include some coverage of five basic topics: (1) psychological sex differences (e.g., in cognitive skills, aggression); (2) biological aspects of sex differences (e.g., the influence of genes, hormones); (3) childhood sex-role socialization, including both empirical data and theoretical perspectives; (4) sex differences in achievement; and (5) sexuality. While authors organize topics in different ways, most review empirical evidence about sex differences in personality and behavior, discuss both biological and social origins of sex differences, and consider the impact of gender on achievement and sexuality. In addition, some texts also include chapters on sex-role stereotypes, minority women, a life-cycle perspective on women's lives, and cross-cultural comparisons.

## A Reader's Guide

Of the ten books we examined, eight are designed as general texts on the psychology of women or sex roles. Two other books by Deaux and by Forisha have a more specialized focus. We begin by discussing each of the general texts.

*Women: A Psychological Perspective* by Donelson and Gullahorn is a comprehensive text. Although only nine of the 16 chapters were written by Donelson or Gullahorn and the rest were contributed by other authors, the book more closely resembles an authored text than an edited volume. The presentation of core topics is supplemented by separate chapters on animal behavior, sex differences in the use of language, friendship, the woman professional, the single woman, and equality and social structure. The authors strike a nice balance between emphasis on intrapsychic and social determinants of behavior. Unlike other books we reviewed, this one is available in hardcover. The book's format includes such features as two columns of text per page; chapter outlines and summaries; extensive use of graphs, diagrams, and tables; and a glossary. Thus, the book more closely approximates a traditional textbook format than any of the others we surveyed. Clear organization, careful documentation, and the inclusion of student aids make this an excellent lower-level undergraduate text, well-suited for a student's first exposure to a solid course on the psychology of women.

*Women and Sex Roles* by Frieze et al. presents the most comprehensive text available. While most books have about 12 chapters, this one has 18. The book is unusual in its detailed and thoughtful discussion of sexist bias in empirical research and in personality theories. Also unusual are chapters on psychological disorders of women, prejudice and discrimination against women, sex differences in the use of power strategies, nonverbal behavior, and political power. The depth of coverage of most topics sets this book apart from the others. For instance, while most books devote a few pages to a cognitive-developmental perspective on sex-role acquisition, Frieze et al. devote a full chapter to the topic. The book is clearly written, with tables and separate boxes containing illustrations. However, the extensive detail and concern with research methods may make the book more suitable for advanced undergraduate courses for psychology majors, rather than for courses attracting students with little background in psychology.

*Half the Human Experience* by Hyde and Rosenberg is a shorter text with 12 chapters. In addition to a discussion of core topics, there are separate chapters on images of women in history and mythology, stages in the life cycle, sex differences in animal behavior, black women, and a cross-cultural perspective. Each chapter ends with a section of conclusions, and some use is made of tables, diagrams, photographs, case histories, and cartoons. The book is somewhat less extensively documented than others. While this makes the text more readable, we sometimes wondered whether the authors were giving undue emphasis to isolated studies or to speculations. For example, we were unclear about the basis for asserting that "girl-groups may have a negative impact on the adolescent girl's developing sense of self" (p. 69) or that "homosexual women live almost an idyllic love relationship with their partner" (p. 176).

*Toward Understanding Women* by O'Leary provides a scholarly, well-documented coverage of topics rather similar to those discussed by Hyde and Rosenberg. In addition to core topics, O'Leary has chapters on stereotypes, a life-span perspective on women's roles, and an excellent chapter on black women (written by Algea Harrison). The book includes summaries of each chapter and a few tables and diagrams. It is written in a clear and organized fashion but, like most texts we reviewed, tends to be rather serious in tone. Although O'Leary acknowledges that the behavior of women and men is "affected by the political and social environment" (p. 202), her book gives little emphasis to these factors, focusing instead on more psychological and intrapersonal analyses. For example, her discussion of women's achievement deals largely with motives and attributions, and says little about social and institutional barriers to achievement.

The Longest War: Sex Differences in Perspective by Tavris and Offir has two unusual features. First, the book is a model of lively presentation of social science fact and theory. The book succeeds in combining scholarship with fascinating examples and occasional humor. Second, the book is somewhat more interdisciplinary than most. Chapters on core topics are supplemented with a sociological perspective on work and marriage, an anthropological perspective on the origins of roles and rituals, and a cross-cultural discussion of sex roles in the Soviet Union, China, Sweden, and Israel. Of the texts we reviewed, this one would be the most easily understood by students with little background in psychology or by lay readers. Because the book is fairly short (nine chapters), it could be used as a basic text for a course on the psychology of women, in conjunction with other readings, or as a supplementary reading in other courses in psychology or women's studies.

Sex Roles: Biological, Psychological and Social Foundations by Weitz is also interdisciplinary. The book is organized around three systems that maintain traditional sex roles: the biological system, the psychological system (sex-role socialization), and the social system (the institutions of work and marriage, and symbolic images of the sexes). While the content of the book resembles that of Tavris and Offir, the style of the two books is markedly dissimilar. Weitz indicates that her book is a personal account of sex roles that makes "no attempt . . . to summarize the vast literature that has been accumulating in the field" (p. 5). Rather, Weitz has "sifted through" the literature to illustrate the workings of the "sex role system." Each chapter is accompanied by footnotes and suggested readings. While individual sections such as the discussion of women's careers are excellent, the book as a whole has several problems. Weitz does a poor job of explaining key concepts, and her prose is often difficult to read. Hence, the usefulness of her analysis of the "sex role system" is limited.

*Sex-Role Psychology* by Frank Wesley and Claire Wesley is the shortest of the texts we reviewed. In addition to core topics, the book includes chapters on vocational differences between the sexes, the assessment of sex differences in interests and in masculinity/femininity, and a discussion of different strategies for achieving "equalization" between the sexes. The book is well-documented, but rather dull and somewhat limited in scope. The book has chapter summaries, but does not include tables, diagrams, or other illustrations.

*Psychology of Women: Behavior in Biosocial Context.* Williams couples a discussion of core topics with heavy emphasis on personality theory and on biology. Her two personality chapters, the first on psychoanalytic theory and the second on Horney, Thompson, Adler, and Mead are both excellent. Four separate chapters are devoted to biological topics, including sexual dimorphism, biology, and behavior; sexuality; birth control; and pregnancy, childbirth, and breast-feeding. Additional chapters concern changing roles for women, emotional disorders and delinquency, and aging. Those who would prefer a text that discusses personality theory and biology in detail will find this book well-organized and clearly written.

*Comparing the texts.* These eight texts vary on several dimensions. A major issue concerns the breadth of topics covered. In this respect, the Frieze et al. book is unique in providing the most detailed and comprehensive text currently available. Donelson and Gullahorn provide a solid but somewhat lower-level text. Those who prefer a somewhat shorter but well-documented presentation of core topics would probably consider the books by Hyde and Rosenberg, O'Leary, and Wesley and Wesley. Our favorite among these three is O'Leary's book, which seems more balanced in content and interpretation than the other two. Readers interested in a short text with an interdisciplinary approach are advised to consider the text by Tavris and Offir. Finally, those who would like a text weighted toward personality and biological approaches should consider the book by Williams.

These eight books also vary considerably in degree of documentation and style of presentation. The books by Frieze et al. and by O'Leary are probably the most detailed in their scholarship; they are useful as professional reference books as well as textbooks for classroom use. Weitz, by intention, has the least documentation. The other books fall somewhere in between, but are generally acceptable in scholarship. Virtually all these texts are rather serious in tone, and lack the use of interesting examples and anecdotes that enliven texts in other areas of psychology. The notable exception is the Tavris and Offir book. Finally, most texts provide few student aids and make limited use of tables, graphs, glossaries and the like to help students understand the text. Here the main exception is the book by Donelson and Gullahorn, which does include such features.

## Special Focus Books

Two of the new books we reviewed are designed for specialized purposes. *The Behavior of Women and Men* by Deaux uses a social-psychological perspective to compare the behavior of adult men and women. The book provides a brief overview of research on stereotypes, self evaluations of men and women, and sex differences/similarities in achievement striving, communication styles, altruism, aggression, cooperation, group behavior, and interpersonal attraction. The organization of the book makes it ideal as a supplement to a course in social psychology. But, since the book reviews material not found in most of the general texts we reviewed, it would also be suitable as supplementary reading in a course on the psychology of women. The book is clear and readable, and does not require any background in psychology to be understood.

Forisha's *Sex Roles and Personal Awareness* is explicitly designed to help readers reexamine how "sex-role expectations obstruct our development as full human beings" (p. 10). The book is humanistic in orientation, and combines brief reviews of research findings with case histories and exercises designed to encourage readers to apply materials to their own lives. Heavy emphasis is given to the impact of sex roles in intimate relationships and marriage. The book makes enjoyable reading, and provides both chapter summaries and a glossary. For those seeking a book with an experiential focus that emphasizes the implications of sex roles for personal growth, this book is a welcome arrival.

## How "Feminist" are the Books?

It has become fashionable in reviewing books on the psychology of women to discuss their degree of "feminism." While reluctant to classify books on this dimension, we can suggest some criteria that might be useful in making such judgments. First, a feminist orientation might be reflected in a discussion of sexist biases in the conduct and interpretation of psychological research, in the development of psychological theories, and in clinical practice. The most extensive coverage of this issue is found in the Frieze et al. book, with shorter discussions (e.g., a critique of Freud) in most of the books.

A second measure of feminism might be the extent to which a book emphasizes social and institutional influences on women's lives, as well as intrapsychic and psychological factors. A feminist analysis of sex roles would thus be both social and psychological in character. For example, in discussing women's achievements, attention would be given to social factors such as job discrimination, as well as to psychological factors such as motives and abilities. Here, high marks would go to Frieze et al., to Donelson and Gullahorn, and to the interdisciplinary books by Tavris and Offir, and by Weitz. Most other texts give more limited attention to social and cultural influences.

A third element in a feminist perspective might be a consideration of options and choices open to both women and men. Most of the books we reviewed have some discussion of changing sex roles, of alternative lifestyles (e.g., lesbianism), or of ways to achieve sex equality. Three books stand out in this regard, however. Frieze et al. devote a separate chapter to personal choices about sex roles. Donelson and Gullahorn have a chapter on the single woman, and discuss options surrounding marriage. Forisha's entire book explicitly encourages readers to question the applicability of traditional roles for their own lives.

A final element in a feminist analysis might be the acknowledgment that power and privilege are key issues in understanding male-female relationships and the realities of women's lives. Frieze et al. devote several chapters to power-related topics. Tavris and Offir, and Weitz also give some mention to this issue, but it is essentially absent from the other books we reviewed.

### Concluding Remarks

Those who have contributed to the development of the psychology of women as an academic field can take pride in the accomplishments of the past decade reflected in these ten textbooks. We've come a long way from the not-so-distant "old days" when instructors struggled to compile suitable readings for courses on women. Basic textbooks now on the market are generally quite good, and will make research and theory in the field more readily accessible to students and other interested readers. Some consensus has appeared about the essential topics in courses on the psychology of women; most texts discuss biological and psychological sex differences, socialization, sexuality, and achievement. It seems likely, however, that as research on women moves in new directions, this definition of "core topics" may also shift. In this concluding section, we consider two general ways in which textbooks in the field might be improved.

First, we would like to see a few more publishers put additional money and energy into textbook development. With the exception of Donelson and Gullahorn's book, the texts we reviewed lack such student aids as chapter outlines, glossaries, key word notations, or colorful charts, graphs, and tables. Such features would be more helpful to students than the clever pictures or quotations that now are in common use. Furthermore, the books we examined are not accompanied by an instructor's manual, test items, or a student guide. Those of us who teach courses on women to large lecture classes would find such aids particularly useful. We hope that at least a few publishers and authors will consider adding such features to their texts.

Second, we would like to see some attention given to currently neglected topics. At present, very little discussion is given to an analysis of the male role in American society, or to the new women's movement as a social movement. As social psychologists we are particularly aware of the limited range of adult behavior discussed in these texts. Little attention is typically given to sex differences in social interaction, group behavior, organizational behavior, nonverbal behavior, or the like. Greater attention might also be paid to the social relationships of men and women, and to the impact of gender on such close relationships as friendship, dating, or marriage. We are not proposing that all texts should include these topics. Indeed, it is probably an asset to have textbooks differing in content, so that individual instructors have flexibility in selecting the book best suited to their own interests. We would, however, like to see even greater diversity than currently exists in the range of topics included in basic texts.

Letitia Anne Peplau and Barbara A. Gutek
University of California, Los Angeles

BATTERED WOMEN: A PSYCHOSOCIOLOGICAL STUDY OF DOMESTIC VIOLENCE.
MARIA Roy (Ed.). New York: Van Nostrand Reinhold, 1977, 404 pp.

With the appearance of Maria Roy's book, psychologists were promised a psychological and sociological study of domestic violence. What we have, however, is a good overview of the issues, for those who are trying to make sense out of such abusiveness, but still less than the original promise. Perhaps the most disappointing area of the book is in its psychological analysis of wife abuse, an analysis that simply perpetuates the stereotyped notion of the masochistic woman - even though the authors encourage us to try to like the concept of female masochism better. Roy, an early leader in the struggle to provide shelter and safety for battered women in New York City, has provided a compendium of articles written by those in the fields of psychiatry, psychology, sociology, neurology, law enforcement, arbitration, legislation, and service programs, who have been studying this problem. The individual articles are erratic in their quality, with some being quite acceptable for the new student to domestic violance and others being too watered down to be meaningful, or too technical to be easily understood. A more serious problem is presented by the lack of cohesion. The book would have profited from Roy adding editorial comments as she moved from one author's views to another. In many cases, she has presented authors whose points of view have been seriously challenged by others in the field, without providing that information for her readers. This leaves novices, in an area where most of us are still learning, with the impression that the views expressed in this book are the only expert opinion available. This is not the case.

Accepting this criticism and keeping it in mind, *Battered Women: A Psychosociological Study of Domestic Violence* is indeed a good beginning analysis of the multi-level complexities facing the battered woman, her family, and those in the helping professions. While it is probably inaccurate to call it a research project, due to its unsystematic methodology, Roy's descriptions of the battered women who pass through her shelter in New York City give an interesting description of who those women are. Terry Davidson's brilliant history, tracing the beginnings of men beating women to the discovery of the male role in procreation and subsequent rise of patriarchial religion, is a breath of feminist analysis. Frank Elliot's treatise on the neurological factors that may be involved in the batterer's loss of control fascinated me, although I wished it was longer and in less technical language. It would be expected that any major anthology of research into domestic violence would include the pioneering efforts fo sociologist Murray Straus and his students Richard Gelles and Suzanne Steinmetz. Unfortunately, the papers fell short of the expectations. They were too condensed and simply inadequate to do justice to both the important work and criticism this team has come under. Gelles merely simplifies his original study of violent families in the early 1970's and dishes it up to us in a rather simplistic and condescending manner. Steinmetz presents her thesis that men too are battered, a fact that most of us doing research in this area are willing to acknowledge. However, it is difficult to harken to her heralding cry, when the data show that less than one percent of all known cases result in the woman battering the man, other than in self-defense. Straus's work, the finest of the trio, is an exceptionally good discussion of preventive mental health strategies to reduce the amount of violence in our society, and thus prevent a new generation of children growing up to model after their parents. His suggestions in clinical treatment strategies, though, would better be left for clinical psychologists to determine.

The treatment in this book of the legal side of woman abuse was similarly uneven. The authors point out the unfairness of the law, the inadequacies of the police, and then suggest better police training and more equitable legislation. They also explore the concept of arbitration as an alternative to prosecution in some domestic disputes. Here again, the book would have been so much richer if the criticisms of each possible solution had been presented side-by-side, so that the reader would not be left thinking that the solutions to this complex problem were just around the corner. As Morton Bard's work, trying to train police to be effective crisis workers, has shown, most police feel that they have neither the inclination nor the talent to be social workers when they answer a potentially dangerous domestic violence call. Rather, they wish they had the power to remove someone from the home immediately and for an extended period of time. Moreover, the lethality statistics indicate this might be the most expedient approach for police to take. New data are suggesting that the number of serious assaults and killings are reduced in cities where there is a battered women's shelter in operation. And, arbitration cannot be successful unless both parties feel that they go into such a negotiation session feeling as equals, which is rarely the case for a battered woman. Roy's inclusion of the controversial "International Association of Chief's of Police Training Keys" provides a revelation of how the police really operate, and will educate everyone about the way it really is out there. So, too, for the copies of good legislation adopted by various states, and the model of service delivery that Roy outlines.

In summary, despite some serious flaws, I recommend *Battered Women: A Psychosociological Study of Domestic Violence* to readers interested in gaining an understanding of many of the salient issues involved in domestic violence. At the same time, I strongly recommend reading Del Martin's book, *Battered Wives* (reviewed in *Psychology of Women Quarterly*, Vol. 2, pp. 286–287) simultaneously, for the balance of perspective. For those graduate students and others interested in deeper analysis of why family members commit violence against one another, I recommend the special Spouse Abuse edition of *Victimology: An International Journal* (Spring 1978), and Chapman's and Gates's *Victimization of Women*, in the Sage Publications Women's Policy Studies Series (Vol. 3, 1978).

Lenore E. Walker
*Colorado Women's College*


VIOLENCE AND THE FAMILY.
John P. Martin (Ed.). New York: Wiley, 1978, 369 pp., $29.25

Family violence has been the skeleton in the attic of domestic life, largely ignored until recently by social agencies and social scientists. Prior to the 1970's, scientists interested in violent behavior concentrated on studies of suicide, homicide, juvenile crime, and violence on television. Psychologists tended to view violence in the family as rare, dysfunctional, or traceable to psychopathy. Now it has been established that violence between family members is more common in the United States than violence between any other individuals except that taking place during wars and riots. The National Commission on the Causes and Prevention of Violence reported that over 25% of males and 17% of females approve slapping a spouse. Eighty-five per cent of American parents use physical punishment on their children. Over 60% of a sample of college students report using physical force on a brother or sister.

These are some of the findings reported by Gelles in *Violence and the Family,* edited by J. P. Martin. Martin, a professor of sociology and social administration at the University of Southampton in England, has compiled this volume. His aim is to present what is known about family violence, to put this knowledge in a psychological and sociological perspective, and to discuss how it affects social policy and practice, as well as the training of social workers facing problems of family violence. The first section presents five brief case studies of women in refuges in England and a chapter reporting a survey of battered wives, largely from Chiswick Women's Aid. The second section includes a review of the literature on child abuse, largely from English sources, a chapter reporting criminal statistics on violence in England, Wales, and Scotland, an historical review of family violence in Great Britain, a sociological perspective, and chapters on violence in the American and the Mediterranean family. The third section on social policy and social action includes chapters on problems facing social workers, on refuges for battered wives, and on issues in training workers.

Because of its avowed focus on family violence and social service administration in England and Wales, the book may have limited interest for American readers, other than from a comparative point of view. However, there are several chapters worthy of attention, notably those by Marsden, on the sociological perspective, and Gelles, on violence in the American family. In addition, the chapters on training raise some important issues. Marsden draws attention to the limitations of the functionalist view, which has led to the family's being regarded as a haven of peace that serves a tension-management function for the wider society. He observes that Straus's model, although emphasizing the learned nature of violence through exposure to examples in the family and the mass media, follows the functionalist tradition of viewing women as continuing in violent relationships because of their personalities, rather than through the weight of external constraints. Marsden is among those who urge consideration of other than physical forms of violence. He points out how the subordination of women (and children) leads women to remain in violent relationships, because of the security and status which a man, any man, confers upon a woman in marriage.

In his chapter, Gelles presents the conflicting norms which simultaneously encourage and approve physical violence and condemn violence in the home. He advocates a multi-dimensional causal model for understanding family violence. It includes such factors as the acceptance of violence in the United States; the stress associated with low economic security, which leads family members to victimize one another; sexual inequality; and social-psychological factors, such as the exposure to violent models in the family, and the lack of social controls due to the privacy of the family.

The usefulness of the section on social policy arises in part from a sympathetic chapter by Roberts in defense of social workers. It graphically presents the problems of the professional worker trying to intervene with child abusing families. A chapter by the North West Region of the National Women's Aid Federation points to the need for workers to examine their own attitudes toward the sanctity of marriage and the family, and become aware of the extent to which they reinforce traditional and oppressive attitudes toward women, including commonly held prejudices against battered women. The chapter which follows nicely illustrates the sexist biases in social work writing alluded to by the Federation.

This volume should be a useful compilation for those concerned with a comparative look at this problem. As is often the case in an edited work, the chapters are uneven and not well integrated. The laudable attempt to relate research to practice is handicapped by the editor's own biases. His concern to preserve the family, and his rejection of structural explanations, such as the status of women and children, in favor of psychological causes of violence, are most apparent in his concluding chapter. Feminists may be surprised by his statement that "in most Western countries the political battle has long been won. Women have risen to the top of almost every profession thus fatally undermining the simple notion of inherent male superiority." Child advocates may question his position that the problem of child abuse is "where legitimate force ends and brutality and cruelty begin."

Rachel T. Hare-Mustin
*Villanova University*

HERE TO STAY: AMERICAN FAMILIES IN THE TWENTIETH CENTURY. Mary Jo Bane. New York: Basic Books, 1976, 195 pp., $11.50 cloth.

Demographic data are cited to refute the idea that the family unit is on the decline. Rather, the family is pictured as vital and persisting. For example, documentation is provided to show that women having smaller families, rather than choosing to be child-free, accounts for declining fertility in the United States. People still want families, but with fewer children. Also, data are provided showing that a greater proportion of children today, compared to the past, now live with at least one parent. People are continuing their interest in parenting. Additionally, it is shown that marriages, and even remarriages, continue to occur at high rates. These and other bits of census data force the conclusion that the family is "still a pervasive and enduring institution."

Having disposed of the myths of family disruption with "hard" census data, the final half of the book considers family policy issues. Legal data provide the main substance of these policy concerns. There is a focus on societal concerns as opposing family privacy. Tension is posited between the several societal goals of 1) gender equality, 2) family responsibility for children, and 3) children's rights of equal access to life's opportunities, *versus* the cherished notions of the family as exempt from intruders. The proposed policies to resolve much of the posited tension include passing the ERA, or extending the Fourteenth Amendment into family law, and establishing a national lifetime insurance policy which covers childhood contingencies as well as those of old age.

Several issues are raised beyond those involving the book's superficial presentation of both demographic data and policy considerations. One of these is the concept of the family acting as the private refuge from society. That concept was heavily promoted in some early family theory such as structural-functionalism. However, other explanations make more sense and one should not naively accept that premise merely because it has become imbedded in some existing conservative legal and religious statements. Persons may desire such a family as their own ideal, but as Jetse Sprey has well articulated, logically, a variety of mechanisms may provide similar unabashed refuge (Sprey, 1969). One might even suggest that we need to be more creative in the design of social mechanisms that protect families from being solely identified as some sort of "id," separate from, but linked to, society. Such creative policy could help strengthen the quality of community life and also make our expectations about family interaction more realistic.

Bane's policy presentations have a tentative and quite bland tone. Perhaps this occurred because relevant psychological, political, sociological and economic literature is omitted. Consideration of the social science literature relevant to family life would have provided some direct and cogent answers for the many questions posed.

Another severe neglect is the lack of understanding of the conflict of interests dimensions of the human personal and societal condition. The vying of self interested parties and groups is a ccnstant volatile aspect of understanding family experience. One such group is the legal profession. The book seems to assume that society as a concept is simply our legal system. That is naive and dangerous for families. The book's benign acceptance of legal concepts as mainly determining family policy completely neglects the notion of contending forces within our pluralistic society, and even gives a credence to existing legal concepts that is not deserved. The legal profession is among the slowest of institutions to reform, and will not as long as lawyers and judges make considerable profit out of family litigation, i.e. divorces, separations, child custody, etc., through a counterproductive "adversary" concept of law. Policy to change the existing legalistic control over family life is not addressed. Simply siad, lawyers should be kicked out of the family relations business becaof of their lack of training and incompetence in understanding interpersonal and familial issues. These should be handled by family relations and counseling professionals. Perhaps a start would include using California's *Conciliation Court Law* (Elkin, 1973) as a model for legislation.

Intelligent focus upon family policy is desperately needed among family scholars to help provide impetus for change at state and national levels. Unfortunately this volume does not advance those efforts nor does it contribute to an understanding of American families.

Gilbert D. Nass
*University of Connecticut*

## REFERENCES

Elkin, M. Conciliation courts: The reintegration of disintegrating families. *The Family Coordinator*, 1973, *22*, 63–71.
Sprey, J. The family as a system in conflict. *Journal of Marriage And The Family*, 1969, *31*, 699–706.

EVERY CHILD'S BIRTHRIGHT: IN DEFENSE OF MOTHERING.
Selma Fraiberg. New York: Basic Books, 1977, xiii+162 pp., $8.95.

Selma Fraiberg, social worker, child psychoanalyst, and prolific writer of books and articles about children, has authored a book with provocative implications for the role of women, child care and social policy. A major thesis of her book is that in order for a child to be nourished and loved and become loving, a mother should remain at home until her child is at least five years of age. Her portrayal of alternative arrangements (especially Day Care) is very pessimistic and even disapproving. She buttresses her position with traditional psychoanalytic theorizing, sociobiological perspectives, selected animal data, and hypothetical case studies of parents and cultures.

In reading the volume, we were filled with a bewildering sense of *deja vu*. This book, published in the late seventies, mirrors ideas (and even myths) prevalent in the late forties. Thus, the book is replete with such adages as: biology is destiny; a "good" mother intuitively knows how to be a "good" mother; to be a working mother is to desert, reject, and do irreparable damage to a child's emotional development. Fraiberg's prescriptive statements regarding motherhood are classic examples of the kinds of indictments that have rendered women vulnerable to a sense of guilt that they are not "good enough" mothers.

Many years ago, Kurt Lewin observed that for every social movement a counter-movement is initiated, and, indeed during these last few years we have witnessed a number of counter-movements regarding affirmative opportunities for minority groups and women. The position taken by Fraiberg appears to fit into the category of a backlash response. Many of her recommendations represent backward steps for the so painfully acquired small gains achieved by women in the third quarter of this century.

The title of the volume reveals the author's major orientation—Motherhood must be defended, presumably against feminism and other movements that draw women into roles other than, or in addition to exclusive mothering. For Fraiberg, the path to motherhood is to re-establish the child's "birthright" to mothering. This argument is incomplete. What constitutes adequate mothering? Are the child's needs the only parameter to be considered in the mother-child interaction? At the psychological level, one could ask: What are the psychological rewards and benefits of mothering to mothers? At the level of social equality, one could point out that the defense of the child's birthright may not be compatible with conditions for equalizing relationships between sexes. Fraiberg's choice is to romanticize children's rights, ignoring the dialectics of the mother-child relationship, and the need to work toward a balance in this relationship.

Fraiberg holds a Dick-and-Jane version of the family: It includes a mother at home, children who are well-behaved, and never sick, and a breadwinner father. Even demographically, this ideal family represents at most 24% of contemporary American families. For the increasing number of American mothers who have entered the work force for economic and personal reasons, child care is an essential need and should constitute an essential component of public policy, potentially supporting and enhancing family life.

Fraiberg chooses to focus on the poor quality of child care, weaving in personal observations that both public and private centers are damaging to the child. Certainly many child care facilities are inadequate. However, the availability of quality child care may not be the only or primary consideration in whether a mother chooses to work or not. Since decision-makers have not focused on alternatives to child care such as policies supportive of part-time work, job-sharing, and maternal subsidies, the issue then becomes how can we make child care centers better places for young children?

Perhaps the most serious limitation of the book is that Fraiberg consistently presents herself as a "scientist" while advocating particular policies. Certainly, social scientists have the prerogative to advocate certain policies based on their values and professional experiences. However, to present oneself as a scientist creates an aura of objectivity that is not fulfilled in her writing. The author's selective use of evidence to support her values, especially reflected in the literature cited on animal and human attachment and the omission of references to evidence incompatible with her views on motherhood, such as that summarized by Michael Rutter in his classic *Maternal Deprivation Reassessed*, reduces the significance of her recommendations.

The role of the scientist is to raise questions, to critically evaluate evidence, and to suggest alternative courses of action—functions we realize raise problems when scientists become involved in the formation of public policy. Fraiberg's blurring of the role of the scientist and the advocate point to the need to reexamine the ambiguous boundaries between social science and social action. We need to be skeptical of using limited knowledge to deal with broad-scale social and philosophical issues, which are not now, nor have been in the past, subject to easy analysis and simple prescriptions.

Fraiberg has offered a point of view along with prescriptions which will affect the lives and morale of many women in our society. We share her point of view regarding the need to examine further child rearing and child caring in our society. However, what she has to say must be closely scrutinized by those of us committed to a psychology of women whose conceptual base is emancipatory and diversified rather than restrictive and singular.

Ruby Takanishi and Norma Deitch Feshbach
*University of California, Los Angeles*

MASCULINITY AND FEMININITY: THEIR PSYCHOLOGICAL DIMENSIONS, CORRELATES, AND ANTECEDENTS.
Janet T. Spence and Robert L. Helmreich. Austin: University of Texas Press, 1978, 297 pp., $14.95.

Leaders in bringing about a new look at our notions of masculinity and femininity, Spence and Helmreich have now published a meaty book which is "part finished product and part progress report." Researchers and teachers will enjoy the cogent discussions which introduce and conclude the monograph as a whole and its three interrelated topics: the conceptualization and measurement of masculinity and femininity, the dimensionalization of achievement motivation, and the influence *on* masculinity, femininity, and achievement motivation of parental attributes and behaviors.

The book centers around the Personal Attributes Questionnaire (PAQ). As most of us know, this instrument features "dual" Masculinity and Femininity scales which show a small positive correlation but includes also a traditionally bimodal M-F scale. Where the M-F scale consists of items considered acceptable in one sex but not in the other, the dual scales consist of items desirable for everyone, but even more valued in one sex than the other. In content, the M-F scale assesses aggressiveness and insensitivity *versus* emotional vulnerability, and the dual scales tap positive aspects of what Bakan termed agency and communion.

Although Spence and Helmreich find it somewhat awkward to have both dual and bimodal scales, they suggest that M-F may relate to a biological sex difference in aggression. The traits which have developed in culture, however, are less polarized, no longer mutually exclusive. In modern society, they say, masculinity and femininity refer to personality attributes and should not be confused with sex-role behaviors, from which they have become largely independent.

Is it better to score high on both of the dual measures of masculinity and femininity than to restrict one's virtues to those of either sex? Spence and Helmreich say that it is not necessarily better, and that though they use the term "androgyny" to describe this pattern of scores, they would prefer to avoid its excess meaning. They are not ready to advocate childrearing practices directed to the moulding of androgynous personalities. Although this opinion shows a familiar scientific caution, one wishes it had been elaborated. If one expects wonders of androgyny, then it is true that masculinity often steals the show. The subjects classified as androgynous usually come out just a bit higher on self-esteem or achievement motivation, but the big difference is between those high and low on masculinity. In fact, when it comes to the number of citations among a sample of scientists, the measure of crude bipolar M-F is the only PAQ scale to relate significantly.

Where androgyny comes out clearly ahead is in students' descriptions of their parents. High school students who are classified as androgynous describe their parents as androgynous, and also as having been authoritative, nurturant, and encouraging of achievement. The case would have been stronger if the data had come from the parents themselves, but how reasonable that raising children should be a place where the androgynous excel! Two parents classified as androgynous or an androgynous father and "feminine" mother are the couple types whose parenting seems most desirable.

After their first studies with the PAQ, Spence and Helmreich were concerned to find whether the positive correlation they had achieved between their Masculine and Feminine scales was a phenomenon restricted to college students in the era following the Women's Movement. They found that in a large sample of high school students and in additional college students and their parents, the correlations among PAQ measures and sex of subject were very similar. Although a considerable part of this stability is surely attributable to the operational definitions of the M, F, and M-F scales, the findings are important in showing that the definitions apply consistently across age groups.

Factor analysis of Spence and Helmreich's measure of achievement motivation reveals four factors of theoretical interest: Work Orientation, Mastery, Competitiveness, and Personal Unconcern (the opposite of "fear of success"). By and large, sex differences in achievement motivation are small, tending to disappear when PAQ category is taken into account. However, there are age and class differences, and particular samples, such as men and women scientists and women athletes, show distinctive patterns on the four factors.

Throughout many findings, the Femininity scale does not seem to correlate very highly with anything. One reason is Spence and Helmreich's emphasis on achievement in work and on self-esteem, which is measured by a scale loaded with agentic items about dominance, confidence, and self-assertion. Another reason may be the narrow blandness of the items scored as Feminine. They almost all have to do with being very warm to people, being very helpful, very gentle, very kind, etc. (One can understand why *some* Femininity contributes to self-esteem scores but not in a linear manner.) Martha White has argued that for feminine character to be adequately measured, a woman's *competencies* in relationships with others need to be assessed. These are surely varied—*charm* for attracting people to a relationship or making it enjoyable, *responsibility* for maintaining the relationship or the group, *discrimination* in giving help or expressing appreciation. Attributes such as these would give the Feminine scale more vitality and maturity.

In Bakan's theory, agency and communion are each destructive and negative when they are "unmitigated" by the other. With this idea in mind, Spence, Helmreich, and their students are beginning to explore unfavorable attributes of masculinity and femininity. Egotism and hostility are unmitigated aspects of agency, they say; but how can communion, the desire to help others, be negative? Here again one feels that the concept of the "feminine principle" may be too narrow. If agency has to do with investing in an independent and assertive ego, communion has to do with investing in relationships. And if so, unmitigated communion is not hard to imagine. It could be dependence, clinging, prudishness, devouring or smothering love, failure to recognize the individuality of self or others.

The distinction between one's same-sex traits "unmitigated" by other-sex traits and one's manifestation of "unmitigated" traits associated with the other sex is somewhat similar to Jung's distinction between "shadow" qualities and those of the (negative) anima or animus. When people are not functioning at an optimum level, he said, there is characteristically a merger or sequence of these negative manifestations. Perhaps we are at a point now where we can study the frequency and distribution of such patterns.

Investigators who are considering the PAQ will find it in Appendix A of this well-organized book, and they will admire its brevity and clarity. It is beyond the scope of this review to discuss pros and cons connected with the bipolar, Likert-type format, categories based on a median split, etc. For the research I do, a shortcoming of the PAQ is that it provides no information on how M, F, and M-F are related to other domains of personality. The work of Berzins et al, Heilbrun, Kanner, Wiggins and Holzmuller, and others indicates that masculinity and femininity can be assessed as dual scales with any general personality inventory. Those of us who choose to use such inventories, however, should remember our debt to Spence, Helmreich, and others who have raised the field's awareness about the many ways of studying personality characteristics in men and women.

Ravenna Helson
University of California, Berkeley

## THE CALIFORNIA SCHOOL OF PROFESSIONAL PSYCHOLOGY
## DEAN OF THE BERKELEY CAMPUS

Applications and nominations are invited for the position of Campus Dean, Berkeley Campus, California School of Professional Psychology. The Berkeley campus is one of four campuses of the California School of Professional Psychology. Other campuses are in Los Angeles, San Diego, and Fresno, and the Central Administrative Offices are in San Francisco. The school grants the Ph.D. in professional psychology with emphases in clincal and community psychology. There are 235 full time graduate students, about half at the masters level and the other half at the doctoral level. The program is four years in length and consists of three trimesters per year. A five year, two semester system is under consideration for Fall, 1980. The campus has 21 core faculty members, comprised of 13 FTE's and a diverse pool of contract instructors who teach about 40 contract courses per term. The Berkeley Campus is accredited by the Western Association for Schools and Colleges. The campus is actively preparing to seek APA accreditation. CSPP was the first autonomous graduate school of professional psychology in the country and continues to provide innovative graduate education that combines field experience and training with classroom instruction. The Ph.D. program requires the completion of an approved doctoral dissertation.

RESPONSIBILITIES: The Campus Dean is the chief executive officer of the campus and rep-directly to the President. Responsibilities include: management of physical, fiscal, and other resources; extramural fiscal development; strategic planning; academic leadership including participaing in faculty recruitment and development; conduct of research and service activities. The Campus Dean represents the campus to the Board of Trustees and the All-School Management Council, as well as to the external community which includes the professional psychological community.

QUALIFICATIONS: Candidates must hold an earned doctoral degree in psychology from an accredited college or university. Demonstrated ability in academic administration knowlededge of psychological education, experience in teaching, securing and adminstering extramural financial support, a record of scholarly and professional achievement, and excellent community relations skills are expected. ABPP status is desirable.

CSPP is an equal opportunity affirmative action employer,
APPLICATION DEADLINE: NOVEMBER 1,1979.
Starting Date is, July 1, 1979, or sooner if possible.
Salary Range is from $35,000 to$45,000 per annum.
Submit applications or nominations to:
CHAIRPERSON
Campus Dean Search Committee, 1900 Addison St.
Berkeley CA, 94704

HO
1206
.P76

The motherhood mandate

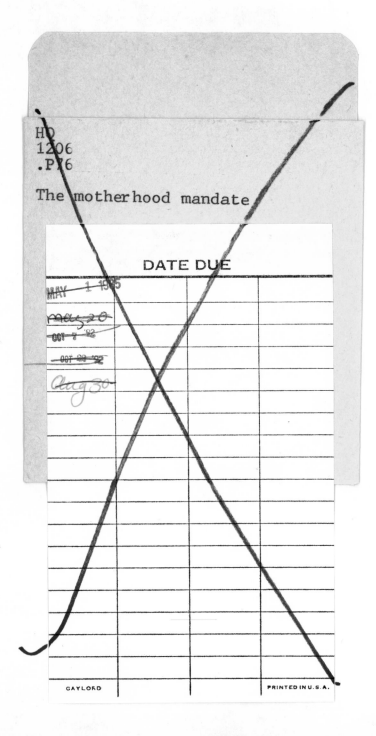